In *the* footsteps *of* Jesus

Resource Manual on Catholic Social Teaching

A Companion to the USCCB Video
In the Footsteps of Jesus: Catholic Social Teaching at Work Today

United States Conference of Catholic Bishops
Washington, D.C.

The project *In the Footsteps of Jesus: Resource Manual on Catholic Social Teaching* was coordinated by the United States Conference of Catholic Bishops (USCCB) Department of Social Development and World Peace and the Catholic Campaign for Human Development in cooperation with Catholic Charities USA, Catholic Relief Services, USCCB Migration and Refugee Services, the National Council of Catholic Women, the Roundtable Association of Diocesan Social Action Directors, and USCCB Publishing. This resource is designed to be used with the USCCB video *In the Footsteps of Jesus: Catholic Social Teaching at Work Today*, which was developed as a follow-up to the 1999 National Catholic Jubilee Justice Gathering. This material has been reviewed by Bishop George V. Murry, SJ, chairman of the Catholic Campaign for Human Development Committee. It is authorized for publication by the undersigned.

Msgr. William P. Fay
General Secretary, USCCB

This guide was written by Dr. Stephen M. Colecchi, who is currently the special assistant to the bishop as well as director of the Office of Justice and Peace of the Catholic Diocese of Richmond in Virginia. He worked for many years in the field of religious education as a parish director of religious education and as a Catholic high school religion teacher. He is also author of *A Leader's Guide to Sharing Catholic Social Teaching* (Washington, DC: USCCB, 2000; publication no. 5-366), which was developed by the USCCB's Committee on Social Development and World Peace and Committee on Education.

Photo credits: cover, Corbis; pp.1, 2, 4, 20, 30, 49, 79, Human Issues Collaborative; p. 38, Margaret (Pegge) Bernecker.

First Printing, July 2004

ISBN 1-57455-499-9

Contents

Introduction

In 1998, the United States Conference of Catholic Bishops (USCCB) (then known as the United States Catholic Conference) issued the statement *Sharing Catholic Social Teaching: Challenges and Directions*. In the document (Washington, DC: USCCB, 1998), the bishops declared, "The sharing of our social tradition is a defining measure of Catholic education and formation." They acknowledged the "commitment and creativity of so many educators and catechists" in sharing Catholic social teaching. But they also observed, "Sadly, our social doctrine is not shared or taught in a consistent and comprehensive way" (3).

In the same year, the bishops issued a reflection on lay discipleship for justice in the new millennium. In their statement *Everyday Christianity: To Hunger and Thirst for Justice* (Washington, DC: USCCB, 1998), they described the laity's social responsibility:

> In these reflections, we highlight one essential dimension of the lay vocation which is sometimes overlooked or neglected: the social mission of Christians in the world. Every believer is called to serve "the least of these," to "hunger and thirst for justice," to be a "peacemaker." Catholics are called by God to protect human life, to promote human dignity, to defend those who are poor, and to seek the common good. This social mission of the Church belongs to all of us. It is an essential part of what it is to be a believer. (1)

In the Footsteps of Jesus is a resource manual designed to accompany the video *In the Footsteps of Jesus: Catholic Social Teaching at Work Today* (Washington, DC: USCCB, 2003). Together with the video, this resource can help parishes enable their parishioners to do the following:

1. Connect Catholic social teaching with the life and ministry of Jesus.
2. Understand seven key themes of Catholic social teaching.
3. Put Catholic social teaching into practice through acts of charity, works of justice, and the pursuit of peace.

The video and this resource manual can be used with individuals of many different ages, including students in grades 7-9, youth in grades 10-12, young adults, and adults. The materials also can be useful for parish councils, committees, ministries, and other groups.

Summary of Part I of the Video

Part I of the video *In the Footsteps of Jesus: Catholic Social Teaching at Work Today* begins by anchoring the Church's social teaching in the person and ministry of Jesus. The video briefly reviews seven key themes of Catholic social teaching and traces the origins of the Church's social teaching in Scripture and its development in the modern era. Part I ends with a compelling challenge to each viewer to act in response to the teaching:

> In the end, however, Catholic social teaching is not about words or documents. These are simply our road maps. Catholic social teaching is really about an invitation. . . . When we are able to find Jesus in our family, in our workplace, and in our community, we are impelled to make our world a better place to live. Take action. Follow in the footsteps of Jesus and share in the magnificent power of Catholic social teaching at work today.

Summary of Part II of the Video

Part II of the video *In the Footsteps of Jesus: Catholic Social Teaching at Work Today* opens with a reminder of Jesus' love and concern for people who are poor, and it links this commitment to our experience of the Eucharist. The challenge of living Catholic social teaching is explored in seven themes: life and dignity of the human person; call to family, community, and participation; rights and responsibilities; option for and with the poor and vulnerable; dignity of work and rights of workers; solidarity; and care for God's creation. Six individuals and a married couple give personal testimonies that illustrate the seven themes. The video closes with examples of how Catholics can use their gifts and talents to make a difference in the world. The examples include both acts of charity and works of justice. Viewers are left with the question, How is God calling *you* to follow in the footsteps of Jesus?

Prayer and Liturgy

Prayer and the liturgy are at the foundation of the Catholic social mission. They inspire Catholics to walk in the footsteps of Jesus. The power of word and sacrament should not be underestimated; it is the power of God. In the memorable words of the Second Vatican Council, "The liturgy is the summit toward which the activity of the Church is directed; at the same time it is the fountain from which all her power flows."[1]

To tap the power of prayer and liturgy more fully, it is important to look at the social meanings of symbols and texts, not just at their personal meanings. Given our individualistic culture in the United States today, this is a challenge. Of course, it would be a mistake to focus exclusively on the social demands of the Gospel and the social mandates of the liturgy. The personal dimensions of both the Gospel and the liturgical mysteries are equally important. Catholics need to balance the social and the personal dimensions of our lives: We are individual persons with personal relationships and struggles. We are also social beings with communal needs and responsibilities.

Liturgical planners, music ministers, and homilists can use this resource manual, *In the Footsteps of Jesus*, to deepen their awareness of Catholic social teaching and to reflect on how to integrate that teaching into prayer and liturgy. Two principles guide the parish in connecting prayer and liturgy with the social mission of the Church. First, the integrity of prayer and liturgy must be respected. Persons committed to social justice must resist the temptation to manipulate prayer and the liturgy. In particular, the parish must avoid any appearance of partisanship. (The "Political Responsibility Guidelines" on page 77 may be helpful in this regard.)

Second, the social demands of the Gospel and Catholic social teaching must be integral to prayer and liturgy. Liturgical planners must resist the temptation to pray prayers and to celebrate liturgies that have little connection to the social dimensions of the Catholic faith and the social needs of our world.

Therefore, we need to have an active partnership between the liturgical and social justice ministries of a parish. Social justice ministers need to respect the expertise of liturgical ministers and to defer to them on the elements of good liturgy.

Liturgical ministers need to defer to the experience of social justice ministers and to craft prayers and liturgies that take into account the social mission and specific social concerns of the parish.

Liturgy

The liturgy itself is social in nature. The community gathers in prayer and is sent forth to the world in mission. The Eucharist is a communal meal to which all are invited. The Eucharist forms the community into the Body of Christ. As a community, we become the One whom we receive in the Eucharist. Our spiritual hunger for God is fed, and we are sent forth to feed a hungry world. We are touched by the real presence of Christ and are sent forth to be the presence of Christ to the world. We experience the real presence of Christ at Eucharist, and our eyes are opened to see the presence of Christ in the poor and the vulnerable. The Eucharist sends us forth to be the "salt and light" of the earth and to be "leaven" in society. The Eucharist enables us to follow in the footsteps of Jesus and to put his teachings into practice in the world.

Following are appropriate ways to highlight the social mission of the Church within the liturgy:

*   *The Word of God*: The starting point for good liturgical planning is the Word of God. The Lectionary is replete with Scriptures that proclaim God's justice and peace. We must look for the social implications of God's Word in addition to the personal implications. This is a challenge in our individualistic culture. Normally the readings of the day are used. This practice ensures that over time God's people are exposed to the entire message of the Gospel (see "The Themes of Catholic Social Teaching and the Lectionary" on page 7).

- *Music:* The selection of music needs to flow from the readings of the day, the season of the year, and the music's function in the liturgy. There are many fine pieces that incorporate the themes of Catholic social teaching since these themes find their origins in God's Word. For example, entrance hymns are meant to intensify the unity of the people gathered and can convey a unity of social purpose. Communion songs enhance the communal nature of the reception of Eucharist and can express our social mission to bring the healing presence of Jesus to the world.

- *Homily:* The homily breaks open the Word of God. When the Scriptures speak of justice, peace, community, poverty, or other aspects of the Church's social teaching, the homilist can illustrate these themes with stories related to contemporary social issues. The homilist can touch on local, state, national, and international concerns. The Preaching the Just Word program at Georgetown University's Woodstock Theological Center provides workshops and resources for how to do this well. The statement *Faithful Citizenship: A Catholic Call to Political Responsibility* of the United States Conference of Catholic Bishops provides a handy summary of the range of social issues of concern to the Church (see page 98 for more information). Dialogue between homilists and the parish social ministry committee can be fruitful in providing the homilist with illustrations and stories related to social issues with which the parish is engaged. The occasion of a second collection for basic human needs—for example, the Catholic Campaign for Human Development or the American Bishops' Overseas Appeal—can provide additional opportunities to make connections between God's Word and the social mission of God's people.

- *General Intercessions:* The Prayer of the Faithful is an obvious time to lift up to God the needs of his people, especially the poor and the vulnerable. It is also a time to pray for peace, justice, and human rights. Those preparing these prayers should have regular communication with the parish's social ministry committee so that these prayers can present social concerns on which the parish is working. Some samples related to the themes of Catholic social teaching are listed below (see "Sample General Intercessions" on page 6).

- *Preparation of the Altar and the Gifts:* Along with the bread and wine for the celebration of the Eucharist, it is appropriate to bring other gifts to fulfill the needs of the

Church and the poor. Special collections at Mass for the needs of the poor connect our sacrifice for others with the sacrifice of Christ. In addition to money, gifts in kind and other substantive gifts for the poor are appropriate, but these do not include token items that will be retrieved and returned to ordinary use after the celebration. It is moving when sign and symbol speak to the themes of Catholic social teaching.

- *Commissioning Ceremonies and Blessings:* At the end of the liturgy or at another time, a special blessing can be offered, or a brief commissioning ceremony can be held, so that the parish community sends forth those who are about to take part in social ministry activities. For example, this can be done before a "Christmas in April" project, or before a parish delegation goes to a Catholic lobby day or leaves to visit a sister parish in another part of the world.

- *Concluding Rite:* The concluding rite sends the community forth to do good works. These good works include both acts of charity and works of justice. Brief announcements are permitted at this time; it is appropriate for these to include invitations to engage in social ministry projects. However, good works include not only the specific social ministry projects of the parish community as a whole, but also the social mission that all believers exercise as family members, workers, owners, managers, investors, consumers, and citizens. The United States Conference of Catholic Bishops' reflection *Everyday Christianity: To Hunger and Thirst for Justice* helps us make these connections (see page 98).

- *Special Liturgies*: The Sacramentary includes "Masses and Prayers for Various Needs and Occasions." The prayers "For Civil Needs" and "For Various Public Needs" can be used on appropriate occasions and serve as models of prayer that are infused with the basic themes of Catholic social teaching. For example, the prayers "For the Progress of Peoples," "For Peace and Justice," and "In Time of War or Civil Disturbance" express human solidarity. The prayers "For Those Unjustly Deprived of Liberty" defend human rights, and those "For the Blessing of Human Labor" express the dignity of work. The latter can be used in conjunction with our nation's celebration of Labor Day. Each year, the United States Conference of Catholic Bishops issues a Labor Day statement that can be used in homily preparation and adult study sessions. It can be found on the website of the USCCB Department of Social Development and World Peace (see page 99).

Here are some examples of other ways—outside of the Mass but connected to liturgy—to reflect the social mission of the parish:

- *Displays*: Many parishes have gathering spaces or common areas just outside the worship space where displays can be set up. The social ministry committee can use this opportunity to prepare visually appealing informative displays regarding special collections or specific social ministry projects or concerns. The displays also can include information sheets that parishioners can take home. The effectiveness of displays will be enhanced if they highlight concerns and projects that the community is reflecting on through the homily, prayers, or music of the liturgy. For example, some parishes prepare informational displays on global development issues in conjunction with the promotion of Operation Rice Bowl during Lent (see page 99).

- *Sign-Up Opportunities*: In conjunction with ongoing displays, or simply set up at tables, the social ministry committee can make sign-up sheets available before or after Mass to recruit volunteers for service or justice projects. Every parish should have opportunities both for acts of charity and for works of justice as responses to the social mission that all share (see "Walking in the Footsteps of Jesus" and "Charity and Justice" for more information).

- *Offerings of Letters*: Some parishes hold "offerings of letters" to public officials on key issues related to the themes of Catholic social teaching. Sometimes parishioners are given sample letters to take home as models for their own letters to public officials. At other times, tables are set up with sample letters, stationery, and postage so that parishioners can compose their letters in an appropriate space after Mass. Sometimes an informational session is held after Mass, or persons involved in social ministry are available to answer questions. This strategy is particularly effective when used on Sundays when the readings of the day provide opportunities for the homilist to use current issues as illustrations of Catholic social teaching in action. Each year, the nonprofit organization Bread for the World provides materials that help parishes make annual offerings of letters on an issue related to hunger. In addition to using such materials, the parish social ministry committee should contact the diocesan social action office or state Catholic conference for guidance on offerings of letters.

- *Adult Study Sessions*: In some parish settings, adults are able to gather after Mass for adult study. This time provides an excellent opportunity to engage parishioners with Catholic social teaching. It is a good time to reflect on the video *In the Footsteps of Jesus*.

NOTE

1. Second Vatican Council, *Constitution on the Sacred Liturgy* (*Lumen Gentium*), 1963, no. 10. In *The Documents of Vatican II*, ed. Walter M. Abbott, SJ (Chicago: Follett Publishing Company, 1966).

General Intercessions

Appendix I of the Sacramentary provides "Sample Formulas for the General Intercessions." Many of these examples incorporate themes of Catholic social teaching. The parish also will want to craft general intercessions that pray for specific needs related to issues and projects being undertaken by its social ministry. Communication between the liturgical and social ministries of the parish is critical in this regard. Below are some additional general intercessions that incorporate themes of Catholic social teaching:

LIFE AND DIGNITY OF THE HUMAN PERSON

For all the peoples of the world, that the Lord will protect the sacred life and dignity of every human person, we pray to the Lord.

For the life and dignity of all God's people, that we may protect life and promote dignity in law and policy, we pray to the Lord.

CALL TO FAMILY, COMMUNITY, AND PARTICIPATION

For our families and our community, that the Lord will strengthen family life and the common good of all, we pray to the Lord.

For our community and nation, that we will learn to embrace the gifts and needs of all, especially the poor and the powerless, we pray to the Lord.

For all citizens, that we will help build a world of justice and peace through our participation in public life, we pray to the Lord.

RIGHTS AND RESPONSIBILITIES

For those who are oppressed, that the Lord will set them free and defend their rights, we pray to the Lord.

For those who suffer injustice, that the Lord will inspire us to champion their rights and to set them free, we pray to the Lord.

OPTION FOR AND WITH THE POOR AND VULNERABLE

For the poor and the vulnerable, that the Lord will lift them up and answer their need through us, we pray to the Lord.

For the voiceless and the powerless, that the Lord will help them find their voices and their power, we pray to the Lord.

DIGNITY OF WORK AND THE RIGHTS OF WORKERS

For all those who labor, that they will have a voice in their work, enjoy the just fruits of their work, and find sustenance for their lives and families, we pray to the Lord.

For all children, especially those in the bondage of child labor, that the Lord will set them free, we pray to the Lord.

SOLIDARITY

For all the nations of the world, that the Lord will help them find the peace and prosperity that flow from authentic solidarity, we pray to the Lord.

For all the peoples of the world, especially those oppressed by poverty, that our nation may walk with them in the journey toward freedom, we pray to the Lord.

CARE FOR GOD'S CREATION

For the beauty of God's creation, that the Lord will gift us with the wisdom to preserve and protect it, we pray to the Lord.

For the earth and all its creatures, that we will treat our planet with the care of a good steward, we pray to the Lord.

The Themes of Catholic Social Teaching and the Lectionary

As noted above, the Lectionary includes numerous Scriptures that communicate the themes of Catholic social teaching. A key to making this connection is to look for the implications of the Scriptures for social practices, policies, laws, and institutions. A skilled homilist is able to infuse his preaching regularly with the social demands of the Gospel. Although the following examples do not constitute a comprehensive index and the same texts also communicate other themes and messages, they illustrate potential links between the themes of Catholic social teaching and the readings of the Lectionary.

THEME	LECTIONARY REFERENCE (CYCLE)
Life and Dignity of the Human Person	Easter Vigil [42] (Year A, Year B, Year C) Fifth Sunday of Lent [34] (A) Fifth Sunday of the Year [74] (A)
Call to Family, Community, and Participation	Sunday in the Octave of Christmas–Holy Family [17] Second Sunday of Easter [44, 45] (A, B) Twenty-Seventh Sunday of the Year [141] (B) Thirty-First Sunday of the Year [153] (B)
Rights and Responsibilities	Third Sunday of the Year [70] (C) Fourth Sunday of the Year [72] (B) Holy Innocents [698] (C) (rights of children to life)
Option for and with the Poor and Vulnerable	Third Sunday of Advent [7] (A) Sixth Sunday of the Year [79] (C) Fifteenth Sunday of the Year [106] (C) Twenty-Sixth Sunday of the Year [139] (C) Twenty-Eighth Sunday of the Year [144] (B)
Dignity of Work and the Rights of Workers	Ninth Sunday of the Year [87] (B) Twenty-Fifth Sunday of the Year [134] (A) Joseph the Worker [559]
Solidarity	First Sunday of Advent [1] (A) Pentecost [63, 64] (A, B, C) Seventh Sunday of the Year [80, 82] (A, C) Twentieth Sunday of the Year [119] (A) Twenty-First Sunday of the Year [153] (B) Christ the King [161] (A)
Care for God's Creation	Eleventh Sunday of the Year [93] (B) Fifteenth Sunday of the Year [104] (A) Francis of Assisi [651]

Sample Prayer Services

n addition to the celebration of the Church's liturgy, individual and group prayer are critical to sustaining a vision and commitment for social justice and peace. As mentioned above, the Sacramentary has a section on "Masses and Prayers for Various Needs and Occasions." The prayers "For Civil Needs" and "For Various Public Needs" found in the Sacramentary can be used on appropriate occasions and serve as models of prayer that are infused with the basic themes of Catholic social teaching.

Below are several prayer services that have been specifically designed for use in groups to reflect on the video *In the Footsteps of Jesus: Catholic Social Teaching at Work Today.*

Instructions for Prayer Services

In settings where it would be appropriate, the environment for group prayer can be enhanced by having an open Bible in a place of honor, perhaps propped on a cloth matching the color of the Church's liturgical season and with candles (if the fire code permits). The reader should be given the reading before the class or session in order to prepare. Ask him or her to read it slowly and with reverence. To enhance the solemnity of the reading, you might ask the reader to reverently use the Bible and to hold it up at the end of the

reading, saying, "The Gospel of the Lord" or "The Word of the Lord," before returning it to its place of honor.

The "Prayer Service on the Seven Themes of Catholic Social Teaching" makes a fitting conclusion for the study of the video and guide. It can be combined with the "Pledge for Charity, Justice, and Peace" for groups who wish to make a commitment to Catholic social teaching at the end of their study. To make the celebration more solemn, the reader of each short Scripture that expresses one of the themes of Catholic social teaching can announce the theme and then light a candle to represent the theme before proclaiming the reading.

Prayer
for the Light of the World

LEADER: Let us place ourselves in the presence of Jesus, the Light of the World.

READER: Now listen to a reading from the Gospel of Matthew. (Reading: Mt 5:13-16) The Gospel of the Lord.

ALL: Praise to you, Lord Jesus Christ.

LEADER: In a world shadowed in the darkness of prejudice and fear of those who are different:

ALL: We are called to be "salt and light."

LEADER: In a world shadowed in the darkness of child labor:

ALL: We are called to be "salt and light."

LEADER: In a world shadowed in the darkness of abortion and disrespect for human life:

ALL: We are called to be "salt and light."

LEADER: In a world shadowed in the darkness of ecological devastation that mars the beauty of God's creation:

ALL: We are called to be "salt and light."

LEADER: Gracious God, you shine the light of faith in our hearts and call us to be the "light of the world" (Mt 5:14). May your light guide us today as we study your will for our world. We ask this through Christ, our Lord.

ALL: Amen.

Prayer
for God's Spirit of Justice

LEADER: Let us place ourselves in the presence of God's Spirit of justice.

READER: Now listen to a reading from the Gospel of Luke. (Reading: Lk 4:18-19) The Gospel of the Lord.

ALL: Praise to you, Lord Jesus Christ.

LEADER: We are sent to bring glad tidings to the poor and to families and communities everywhere:

ALL: The Spirit of the Lord is upon us.

LEADER: We are sent to proclaim liberty to those whose lives are threatened and whose rights are denied:

ALL: The Spirit of the Lord is upon us.

LEADER: We are sent to recover sight for the blind and to see the beauty of God's creation:

ALL: The Spirit of the Lord is upon us.

LEADER: We are sent to let oppressed workers go free and to defend the rights of the poor:

ALL: The Spirit of the Lord is upon us.

LEADER: We are sent to proclaim God's Reign of justice and peace in solidarity with all nations:

ALL: The Spirit of the Lord is upon us.

LEADER: Gracious God, you have sent your Spirit upon us so that we might be your presence in our world. May your Spirit be upon us today as we study your will for our world. We ask this through Christ, our Lord.

ALL: Amen.

Prayer
for Light in the Darkness

LEADER: Let us place ourselves in the presence of our God, the Light in the darkness of our world.

READER: Now listen to a reading from the prophet Isaiah. (Reading: Is 58:6-10) The Word of the Lord.

ALL: Thanks be to God.

LEADER: Release those bound unjustly. Set free the oppressed:

ALL: Then light shall rise in the darkness.

LEADER: Share your bread with the hungry. Shelter the homeless:

ALL: Then light shall rise in the darkness.

LEADER: Clothe the naked. Do not turn your back on those in need:

ALL: Then light shall rise in the darkness.

LEADER: Then your light shall break forth like the dawn:

ALL: Then light shall rise in the darkness.

LEADER: Remove from your midst oppression and false accusation:

ALL: Then light shall rise in the darkness.

LEADER: Bestow your bread on the hungry and satisfy the afflicted:

ALL: Then light shall rise in the darkness.

LEADER: Gracious God, you are the Light of the World and you call us to be light in the darkness of our world. Help us to respond to your call with generous hearts and steadfast justice. We ask this through Christ, our Lord.

ALL: Amen.

Prayer Service

on the Seven Themes of Catholic Social Teaching: Our Call, Our Tradition

LEADER: Let us place ourselves in the presence of the God who calls us to be "salt and light."

READER: A reading from the Gospel of Matthew. (Reading: Mt 5:14-16)

ALL: The Church's social teaching is a rich treasure of wisdom about building a just society and living lives of holiness amid the challenges of modern society.

Life and Dignity of the Human Person
READER: A reading from the Book of Genesis. (Reading: Gn 1:27)

ALL: The Catholic Church proclaims that human life is sacred and that the dignity of the human person is the foundation of a moral vision for society. . . . We believe that . . . the measure of every institution is whether it threatens or enhances the life and dignity of the human person.*

Call to Family, Community, and Participation
READER: A reading from the Book of Exodus. (Reading: Ex 6:7)

ALL: The person is not only sacred but also social. How we organize our society in economics and politics, in law and policy directly affects human dignity and the capacity of individuals to grow in community.*

Human Rights and Responsibilities
READER: A reading from the prophet Isaiah. (Reading: Is 10:1-2)

ALL: The Catholic tradition teaches that human dignity can be protected and a healthy community can be achieved only if human rights are protected and responsibilities are met. Therefore, every person has a fundamental right to life and a right to those things required for human decency.*

*Excerpts are from Sharing Catholic Social Teaching: Challenges and Directions. Reflections of the U.S. Catholic Bishops (Washington, DC: USCCB, 1998).

Option for and with the Poor and Vulnerable

READER: A reading from the Acts of the Apostles. (Reading: Acts 2:44-45)

ALL: A basic moral test is how our most vulnerable members are faring. In a society marred by deepening divisions between rich and poor, our tradition . . . instructs us to put the needs of the poor and vulnerable first.*

Dignity of Work and the Rights of Workers

READER: A reading from the Book of Sirach. (Reading: Sir 34:22)

ALL: The economy must serve people. . . . Work is more than a way to make a living; it is a form of continuing participation in God's creation. If the dignity of work is to be protected, then the basic rights of workers must be respected.*

Global Solidarity

READER: A reading from the prophet Micah. (Reading: Mi 4:3)

ALL: We are our brothers' and sisters' keepers. We are one human family, whatever our national, racial, ethnic, economic, and ideological differences. Learning to practice the virtue of solidarity means learning that "loving our neighbor" has global dimensions in an interdependent world.*

Care for God's Creation

READER: A reading from the Book of Genesis. (Reading: Gn 1:31)

ALL: We show our respect for the Creator by our stewardship of creation. We are called to protect people and the planet, living our faith in relationship with all of God's creation. This environmental challenge has fundamental moral and ethical dimensions that cannot be ignored.*

Conclusion: Seeing as God Sees

READER: A reading from the Gospel of John. (Reading: Jn 9:39-41)

LEADER: Our tradition calls us to see the world in new ways—to reject the blindness of our age. And so we pray. We are called to see with the eyes of the poor in a world blinded by riches and power.

ALL: Cure our blindness, O God.

LEADER: We are called to see with the eyes of the outcast, the person suffering with leprosy, the person living with HIV/AIDS in a world blinded by fear.

ALL: Cure our blindness, O God.

LEADER: We are called to see with the eyes of all God's creatures in a world blind to the beauty of God's creation.

ALL: Cure our blindness, O God.

LEADER: Jesus has opened our eyes to the needs of God's world.

ALL: We are ready to open our hands to God's work.

LEADER: Jesus has opened our minds to the injustices of the world.

ALL: We are ready to open our mouths to proclaim God's justice.

Pledge for Charity, Justice, and Peace

Offices of the United States Conference of Catholic Bishops and other national Catholic organizations originally promoted the *Jubilee Pledge for Charity, Justice, and Peace* as a practical response to the Holy Father's designation of 1999 as "the year of charity." But the pledge itself retains an abiding value in the third millennium. Individuals or groups can use the pledge to mark their commitment to live the themes of Catholic social teaching. The pledge can be used separately or in the context of a prayer service, for example, at the conclusion of the "Prayer Service on the Seven Themes of Catholic Social Teaching" on pages 12-14.

Pledge for Charity, Justice, and Peace
A Catholic Commitment for the Third Millennium

The Jubilee of our Lord's birth calls us "to bring glad tidings to the poor, to proclaim liberty to captives, recovery of sight to the blind, and release to prisoners" (Lk 4:18).

AS DISCIPLES OF JESUS IN THE THIRD MILLENNIUM, I/WE PLEDGE TO

PRAY regularly for greater justice and peace.

LEARN more about Catholic social teaching and its call to protect human life, stand with the poor, and care for creation.

REACH across boundaries of religion, race, ethnicity, gender, and disabling conditions.

LIVE justly in family life, school, work, the marketplace, and the political arena.

SERVE those who are poor and vulnerable, sharing more time and talent.

GIVE more generously to those in need at home and abroad.

ADVOCATE public policies that protect human life, promote human dignity, preserve God's creation, and build peace.

ENCOURAGE others to work for greater charity, justice, and peace.

Signature

"Love for others, and in the first place love for the poor, in whom the Church sees Christ himself, is made concrete in the promotion of justice." (Pope John Paul II, Encyclical letter *On the Hundredth Anniversary of "Rerum Novarum"* [*Centesimus Annus*] [Washington, DC: USCCB, 1991])

Education and Catechesis

In their 1998 statement *Sharing Catholic Social Teaching: Challenges and Directions*, the Catholic bishops of the United States declare:

Catholic schools, religious education, adult education, and faith formation programs are vitally important for sharing the substance and values of Catholic social teaching. Just as the social teaching of the Church is integral to Catholic faith, the social justice dimensions of teaching are integral to Catholic education and catechesis. (6)

This resource, *In the Footsteps of Jesus*, provides tools for integrating catechesis on seven key themes of Catholic social teaching into catechetical and educational programs for youth and adults. This guide includes outlines for educational sessions for grades 7-9, grades 10-12, young adults, and adults. These sessions can be used in a wide range of parish educational settings, including the following:

- Catholic schools
- catechetical programs
- youth ministry
- adult education
- small faith communities (adult faith-sharing groups)
- young adult ministry
- catechumenate sessions
- Confirmation preparation

Three principles should guide the parish in connecting Catholic education and catechesis with learning more about the social mission of the Church:

1. The expertise of educators should be respected and used. Social justice leaders should resist the temptation to share the wealth of information that they have on social issues in ways that do not match the learning styles of youth and adults. They should also resist the urge to set up separate educational events on social justice. Sharing Catholic social teaching needs to be part of the mainstream curriculum of the parish at all levels. An occasional special program or speaker on social justice is fine, but too often these programs operate at the margins of the parish and attract the "usual suspects."

2. The experience and expertise of those in social justice ministry should be respected. Educational and catechetical ministers must resist the temptation to create their own outlets for acts of charity and works of justice. As every good educator knows, the real test of knowledge is putting it into practice, but those in the parish's catechetical ministries should consult with those in the parish's social justice ministry to find opportunities to act on the Church's social mission. These opportunities should include both service projects (charity) and justice projects (social transformation). See the discussions of charity and justice and the "ART" of Catholic social teaching in "Walking in the Footsteps of Jesus" on pages 70-73.

3. The parish's educational and catechetical programs should avoid any appearance of partisanship or unproductive ideological disputes. The "Avoiding Ideological Conflicts" ground rules on page 76 and the "Political Responsibility Guidelines" on page 77 are helpful in this regard.

An active partnership between the educational and social justice ministries of a parish can strengthen both ministries. Social justice ministers need to respect the expertise of catechetical ministers and to defer to them on sound educational methods. Educational ministers need to defer to the experience of social justice ministers and need to highlight issues and craft service and justice projects that take into account the social mission and the specific social concerns of the parish.

Training of Catechetical and Educational Leaders

The task of equipping parish catechetical and educational leaders to share and act on social teaching deserves special attention. In addition to the *In the Footsteps of Jesus* video and resource manual, leaders can consult the *Leader's Guide to "Sharing Catholic Social Teaching"* (Washington, DC: USCCB, 2000), a flexible resource that can be used to train educational and catechetical leaders for the task of infusing Catholic social teaching consistently into their teaching, programs, and activities for all age levels. The manual is designed for parish directors of religious education and catechists, Catholic school principals and teachers, Rite of Christian Initiation of Adults leaders and teams, youth and young adult ministry leaders, and those engaged in sacramental preparation and a range of other activities that form people in faith.

Social Ministry

The Catholic bishops of the United States reflected on the social mission of the parish in their 1993 statement *Communities of Salt and Light: Reflections on the Social Mission of the Parish* (Washington, DC: USCCB, 1994). In the document, the bishops stated:

> Effective social ministry helps the parish not only do more, but be more—more of a reflection of the gospel, more of a worshipping and evangelizing people, more of a faithful community. It is an essential part of parish life. (1)

They further argued for a "framework of integration" to keep social ministry at the heart of parish life. They maintained:

> We need to build local communities of faith where our social teaching is central, not fringe; where social ministry is integral, not optional; where it is the work of every believer, not just the mission of a few committed people and committees. (4)

Within this framework of integration, the parish's social ministry leaders and committees play a pivotal role. Their task is to analyze social issues and needs in light of Catholic social teaching and to provide opportunities for parishioners to live this teaching through acts of charity and works of justice. The leaders' job is not to do social ministry for the parish, but to enable the parish to do social ministry.

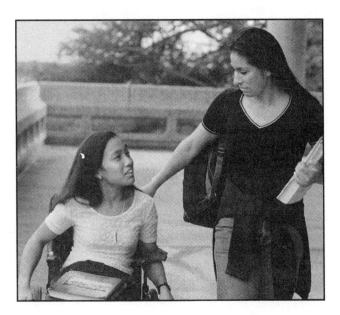

The video *In the Footsteps of Jesus: Catholic Social Teaching at Work Today* and this guide can help the social ministry leaders of the parish to root themselves and their work in the basic themes of Catholic social teaching. To the extent that these teachings are widely held in the parish, parishioners will be drawn to volunteering for parish social ministry projects and to living the social mission in their everyday lives.

Several principles should guide the parish's social ministry work:

1. BE CAREFUL TO SECURELY ROOT ALL SOCIAL MINISTRY PROGRAMS AND PROJECTS EXPLICITLY IN THE THEMES OF CATHOLIC SOCIAL TEACHING. This explicit connection helps to minimize unproductive ideological disputes. (See "Avoiding Ideological Conflicts" on page 76 for more information.) Making this connection also takes advantage of the opportunity every social ministry program presents to help participants learn more about Catholic social thought.

2. COLLABORATE WITH THE PARISH'S LITURGICAL MINISTRY. Share information with liturgical planners so that the entire community can pray for the concerns and projects of the parish's social ministry on a regular basis. (See "Prayer and Liturgy" on pages 3-5 for additional suggestions regarding this partnership.)

3. COLLABORATE WITH THE PARISH'S EDUCATIONAL MINISTRIES. Be ready to recommend social issues to study in light of Catholic social teaching. Make recommendations for service projects (charity) and justice projects (social transformation) that classes, youth groups, and adult study groups can undertake. (See the sections on "Education and Catechesis" and "Charity and Justice" on pages 16 and 70 for additional suggestions for this partnership.)

4. **COLLABORATE WITH THE DIOCESAN SOCIAL ACTION OFFICE, THE STATE CATHOLIC CONFERENCE (IF ONE EXISTS IN YOUR STATE), AND NATIONAL CATHOLIC ORGANIZATIONS.** Other communities have faced many of the same issues and concerns that a parish faces locally. In addition, issues at the state, national, and international levels deeply impact the local parish. Finally, if parishes are to be faithful to the universal nature of the Church, local social ministry efforts must be connected to those of the wider Church.

5. **NURTURE THE LAY MISSION TO THE WORLD.** Do not compete with it. Parishioner involvement in parish social-ministry activities serves as an encouragement and sign of a wider commitment. Parishioners are also called to live the Church's social teaching in all that they do as family members, workers, owners, managers, investors, consumers, and citizens. The formal social-ministry programs of the parish do not exhaust the social mission of lay disciples.

6. **CONSISTENTLY ENGAGE PARISHIONERS IN BOTH ACTS OF CHARITY AND WORKS OF JUSTICE.** Charity and justice are incomplete without one another. See the discussion on charity and justice and the "ART" of justice and peace in the section on "Walking in the Footsteps of Jesus" (page 70) for more information.

Parish social ministry leaders can use the *In the Footsteps of Jesus* video and this resource manual in a number of ways with people involved in the social mission of the parish. The sessions described in this resource manual can be used with social ministry committee members, direct service program volunteers (e.g., food pantry, clothing closet, and soup kitchen), legislative advocates (in the parish, diocesan, or state legislative advocacy network), community organizers and members of low-income community groups (such as those involved in Catholic Campaign for Human Development projects), Operation Rice Bowl coordinators, respect life ministries, parish peace groups, St. Vincent de Paul societies, and a host of others directly involved in the social mission of the parish.

Other Parish Uses

P arishes can "think outside the box" in using the video *In the Footsteps of Jesus: Catholic Social Teaching at Work Today* and session outlines in this resource manual. Not only can they be used in traditional educational settings, but other parish groups, committees, and councils also can benefit from the video and related program. Here are some suggestions:

- The PARISH COUNCIL could study the themes of Catholic social teaching at regular meetings or on a retreat to help representatives discern parish priorities and give feedback to the parish's social ministry.

- The PARISH FINANCE COUNCIL could do likewise to guide members in their role as stewards of the parish's resources and facilities. The themes of Catholic social teaching also have implications for employment policies, energy savings, socially responsible investment, and purchasing policies, among other dimensions of parish life.

- The parish's SCHOOL BOARD could study the themes and their implications for scholarship policies, curriculum guidelines, employment policies, school mission, and so forth.

- The parish COMMITTEES FOR EDUCATION, LITURGY, AND SOCIAL MINISTRY could study the themes and their implications for effective collaboration among the ministries, as noted in the respective sections of this guide related to these ministries.

The wide range of other PARISH GROUPS to consider include the following:

- Men's and women's groups looking to deepen their mission

- Boy Scout and Girl Scout troops preparing for service and justice projects

- Senior citizens groups who have time for study and legislative advocacy

- Any other group that wants to express this essential dimension of Catholic faith

Sample Sessions
and Outlines

for Grades 7-9

Session One

Anchoring Catholic Social Teaching in the Footsteps of Jesus

TOTAL TIME: 1 HOUR

PREPARATION

Read over this sample outline, the summary of Part I of the video on page 1, and the essay "Overview of Catholic Social Teaching" on pages 50-52. Preview Part I of the video *In the Footsteps of Jesus: Catholic Social Teaching at Work Today.* Copy the "What Did Jesus Teach?" Scripture passages on papers of different colors for each team. Cut slips of paper so that each slip has one Bible passage. Place an open Bible at the front of the classroom in a place of honor, perhaps propped on a cloth matching the color of the Church's liturgical season and between candles (if the fire code permits). Decide ahead of time on a simple and quick way to divide the class into teams of four to six persons. You might make color-coded nametags for this purpose. Place and test the television/video player and have the video set to the start of the tape. Select a reader and leader for prayer.

OPENING PRAYER
4 minutes

Welcome your students. Give any instructions related to the prayer time. Ask them to place themselves in the presence of the Lord. See "Prayer for the Light of the World" on page 9.

INTRODUCTION
5 minutes

Tell your students that today's lesson is about Jesus and his call to transform our world. Ask these or similar questions:

1. Which of the teachings of Jesus would help us to build a better world?
2. Which of these teachings of Jesus do you find difficult to put into practice?

Encourage your students to share brief answers to these questions out loud with the class. Thank the more vocal students for their answers and then ask for anyone who has not spoken to add reflections. Depending on the nature of the group, you might even call upon quieter students by name.

INTRODUCE THE VIDEO *1 minute*

Use the brief description on page 1 of this resource manual to introduce Part I of the video *In the Footsteps of Jesus: Catholic Social Teaching at Work Today.* Ask the students to look for examples of the teaching of Jesus in the video and of how the Church has applied this teaching to our world today.

VIEW PART I OF THE VIDEO *9 minutes*

DEBRIEF/REVIEW THE VIDEO *11 minutes*

Use the questions below to help your students recall some of the major points covered by the video. Simply present the questions to the whole group, asking them to keep their responses brief. (This is not a time for discussion; the goal is to review briefly the content of the video.) Give quieter members of the class an opportunity to contribute. Affirm vocal individuals, and then gently redirect your attention to allow other students to join in.

Questions for Reviewing Part I of the Video
1. What teachings of Jesus are mentioned in the video?
2. Which of today's social issues are mentioned in the video?
3. Which key themes of Catholic social teaching can you remember?

"WHAT DID JESUS TEACH?" EXERCISE

20 minutes

The purpose of this exercise is to show students that Jesus' teachings have relevance to today's social issues. See the instructions on page 80.

FINAL THOUGHTS

8 minutes

Give each group back its passages. Ask the students to look over the teachings of Jesus on the slips of paper. Invite each student to select one teaching that he or she believes our world needs to put into practice at this time. Have each of them share why they selected the passage with the others in the small group or with the whole class as time permits.

CLOSING PRAYER

2 minutes

Remind your students that they are called to be the "light of the world" (Mt 5:14) and to spread the light of Jesus' teachings. Note that we pray for the coming of God's Kingdom and for God's will to be done on earth each time we pray the Lord's Prayer. Lead the class in closing with the Our Father.

Session Two
Exploring the Themes of Catholic Social Teaching

TOTAL TIME: I HOUR

PREPARATION

Read over the following sample outline, the summary of Part II of the video on page 2, and the essay "Seven Themes of Catholic Social Teaching" on pages 53-54. Preview Part II of the video *In the Footsteps of Jesus: Catholic Social Teaching at Work Today*. Make copies of the "Catholic Social Teaching Multiple Choice Quiz" from page 90 for each member of the class. Make available pencils with erasers for each student. Place an open Bible at the front of the classroom in a place of honor, perhaps propped on a cloth matching the color of the Church's liturgical season and between candles (if the fire code permits). Place and test the television/video player and set the video to the start of the Part II of the tape. (Advance tape to 10:36 minutes.) Select a reader and leader for prayer.

OPENING PRAYER

4 minutes

Welcome your students. Give any instructions related to the prayer time. Ask them to place themselves in the presence of the Lord. See "Prayer for God's Spirit of Justice" on page 10.

INTRODUCTORY QUIZ

5 minutes

Tell your students that today's lesson will focus on the seven themes of Catholic social teaching. The Church has identified these themes based on the teaching of Jesus, the foundation of the Scriptures, and the aid of the Holy Spirit. Pass out copies of the "Catholic Social Teaching Multiple Choice Quiz." Ask the students to circle one answer to each of the ten questions. Tell them that they will have an opportunity to change their answers after they view the video. (This is not a test; it is an opportunity to measure their knowledge and learn.)

INTRODUCE THE VIDEO *1 minute*

Use the summary of Part II of the video. Ask the students to look for the seven themes of Catholic social teaching and for the answers to the quiz.

VIEW PART II OF THE VIDEO *19 minutes*

DEBRIEF/REVIEW THE VIDEO *4 minutes*

Use the questions below to help your students recall some of the major points covered by the video. Simply present the questions to the whole group, asking them to keep their responses brief. (This is not a time for discussion; the goal is to review briefly the content of the video.) Give quieter members of the class an opportunity to contribute. Affirm vocal individuals, and then gently redirect your attention to allow other students to join in.

Questions for Reviewing Part II of the Video

1. The video included seven testimonies by individuals and a couple who have lived Catholic social teaching. Which testimony did you find particularly moving and why?
2. Which key themes of Catholic social teaching can you remember?

CATHOLIC SOCIAL TEACHING MULTIPLE CHOICE QUIZ *15 minutes*

Give your students a few minutes to look over their answers to the quiz. Allow them to make changes before you review the correct answers with them. Do not give them the correct answers all at once. Go over each question in order, presenting the correct and incorrect answers as you review the quiz. (The correct answers are on page 91.) For each question, explore the following questions:

1. What is the correct response and why?
2. Why are the other responses incorrect?
3. Have they heard ideas similar to these responses before? (Many of the incorrect responses are based on common misconceptions from today's individualistic and materialistic culture.)

SEVEN THEMES OF CATHOLIC SOCIAL TEACHING *10 minutes*

Use the following information to introduce this section to your students. Also pass out the essay "Seven Themes of Catholic Social Teaching" on page 53.

The life and teaching of Jesus is the foundation of the Church's social teaching, but over the centuries the Church, inspired by the Holy Spirit, has developed a body of social teaching that guides Catholics as we work for a better world. The Catholic bishops of the United States have identified seven key themes of Catholic social teaching.

Using the "Catholic Social Teaching Multiple Choice Quiz," invite your students to make connections between these themes and questions in the quiz. Following are the most obvious connections:

Quiz Question:	Theme:
1	1. Life and Dignity of the Human Person
2	2. Call to Family, Community, Participation
3	2. Call to Family, Community, Participation
4	3. Rights and Responsibilities
5	4. Option for and with the Poor and Vulnerable
6	5. Dignity of Work/Rights of Workers
7	5. Dignity of Work/Rights of Workers
8	6. Solidarity
9	7. Care for God's Creation
10	The call to act on all the themes

CLOSING PRAYER

2 minutes

Remind your students that they are given the gift of the Holy Spirit to help them transform the world by putting the themes of Catholic social teaching into practice. Note that we pray for the coming of God's Kingdom and for God's will to be done on earth each time we pray the Lord's Prayer. Lead the class in closing with the Our Father.

Session Three
Walking in the Footsteps of Jesus

TOTAL TIME: 1 HOUR

PREPARATION

Read over this sample outline and "Walking in the Footsteps of Jesus," including the section on charity and justice on pages 70-72. Preview the last segment of Part II of the video *In the Footsteps of Jesus: Catholic Social Teaching at Work Today*, starting at 25:00 minutes. Read over the "Stand Up If . . ." exercise on pages 92-95 and decide what portions of it to use with your group. Contact your parish's social ministry committee to select a service or justice project for your class to undertake. (Note: Over time, it is important to give students experiences with both types of responses to Catholic social teaching.) Place and test the television/video player; set the video to start at the last segment of the tape after the seventh theme in Part II. (Advance the tape to 25:00 minutes.) Have a board or flip chart ready to use. Select a reader and leader for prayer.

OPENING PRAYER

4 minutes

Welcome your students. Give any instructions related to the prayer time. Ask them to place themselves in the presence of the Lord. See "Prayer for Light in the Darkness" on page 11.

INTRODUCTION

6 minutes

Tell your students that today's lesson is about responding to Catholic social teaching and walking in the footsteps of Jesus. Ask these or similar questions:

1. Many of the teachings of Jesus would help us to build a better world. What are some of the teachings of Jesus that we looked at in past sessions?

2. The Holy Spirit has inspired the Church to build upon the foundation of Jesus' teachings and to develop Catholic social teaching. What major themes of Catholic social teaching can you remember?

Encourage your students to share brief answers to these questions out loud with the class. Thank the more vocal students for their answers and then ask for anyone who has not spoken to add reflections. Depending on the nature of the group, you might even call upon quieter students by name.

"STAND UP IF . . ." EXERCISE *16 minutes*

Use the instructions for the "Stand Up If . . ." exercise on page 92. Debrief. The purpose of this exercise is to show the group that all of us have opportunities to put Catholic social teaching into practice.

INTRODUCE THE VIDEO *1 minute*

Tell the class that they have already seen Part II of the video *In the Footsteps of Jesus*. Indicate that you are going to show them only the final segment of the video, which suggests ways that we can put into practice the themes of Catholic social teaching.

DEBRIEF/REVIEW THE VIDEO *8 minutes*

Use the following questions to help your students recall some of the major points covered by the video. Simply present the questions to the whole group, asking them to keep their responses brief. (This is not a time for discussion; the goal is to review briefly the content of the video.) Give quieter members of the class an opportunity to contribute. Affirm vocal individuals, and then gently redirect your attention to allow other students to join in.

Questions for Reviewing the Final Segment of Part II of the Video
1. When asked what to do to make a difference in the world, what advice did Blessed Teresa of Calcutta offer? ("Just do what's in front of you.") What did she mean? What is in front of us?
2. The video mentioned a number of ways to put Catholic social teaching into practice. What were some of the ways that the video mentioned?

CHARITY AND JUSTICE *10 minutes*

Use the material on charity and justice on pages 70-73 to explain the basic distinction to your students. Here is a chart that may help:

Charity:	Justice:
Focuses on the needs of people	Focuses on the rights of people
Looks at individual situations	Analyses social situations or structures
Meets immediate needs	Works for long-term social change
Ameliorates symptoms of social problems	Addresses underlying social causes
Relies on the generosity of donors	Relies on just laws and fair social structures

Next draw a vertical line down the center of the board or flip chart. Title the left side "Charity" and the right side "Justice." Ask your students to list ways to put Catholic social teaching into practice. (Hint: They can draw upon the examples from the video.) Place examples of charity in the left column and examples of justice in the right column.

SERVICE OR JUSTICE PROJECT *10 minutes*

Describe the service project or justice project that was recommended by your parish's social ministry committee. Make sure it is within the capability of your students. Secure parental permission for projects off-site. Over time, try to engage your students in both service and justice projects. For example, one time they might serve a meal in a soup kitchen or collect food for low-income families—a charitable service project. The next time they might write to members of the U.S. Congress about world hunger and foreign aid—a justice project.

CLOSING PRAYER *2 minutes*

Remind students that Jesus is the Light of the World, and that they are called to bring light to the world, too. Note that we pray for the coming of God's Kingdom and for God's will to be done on earth each time we pray the Lord's Prayer. Lead the class in closing with the Our Father.

Outline

for Additional Sessions for Grades 7-9

TOTAL TIME: 1 HOUR

INTRODUCTION

A more in-depth session on one of the seven themes of Catholic social teaching can be designed using the following generic outline.

PREPARATION

For background before the session, read the "Essay" and "Scripture and Tradition" sheets related to the theme you have chosen to explore in greater depth. These can be found on pages 55-69. Preview the segment of Part II of the video *In the Footsteps of Jesus: Catholic Social Teaching at Work Today* related to the theme. The time segments are as follows:

Advance tape to:	Theme:
11:35 minutes	Life and Dignity of the Human Person
14:42 minutes	Call to Family, Community, and Participation
16:45 minutes	Rights and Responsibilities
18:02 minutes	Option for and with the Poor and Vulnerable
19:45 minutes	Dignity of Work and the Rights of Workers
21:40 minutes	Solidarity
23:16 minutes	Care for God's Creation

Place and test the television/video player; set the video to start at the beginning of the appropriate segment.

PRAYER *3 minutes*

Open with a short prayer based on the corresponding theme from "Prayer Service on the Seven Themes of Catholic Social Teaching" on pages 12-14.

INTRODUCE THE VIDEO *1 minute*

Use the brief description of the theme from the "Seven Themes of Catholic Social Teaching" handout on pages 53-54 to introduce the segment of Part II of the video *In the Footsteps of Jesus*.

VIEW THE THEME'S SEGMENT FROM PART II OF THE VIDEO

DEBRIEF/REVIEW THE VIDEO *10 minutes*

Use the questions below to help the participants recall some of the major points covered by the video. Simply present the questions to the whole group, asking them to keep their responses brief. (This is not a time for discussion; the goal is to review briefly the content of the video.) Give quieter members of the group an opportunity to contribute. Affirm vocal individuals, and then gently redirect your attention to allow other participants to join in. Use the background material to fill out their understanding of the theme.

Questions for Reviewing the Video Segment

1. What visual image from the video best captured the theme for you?
2. How would you put the theme into your own words?

Select an activity below related to the themes of Catholic social teaching.

Life and Dignity of the Human Person

Bring a pile of newspapers to class. Divide the class into small groups. Give each group an equal number of newspapers. Ask each group to look for and cut out articles that show how human life and dignity is protected or threatened. Have the students put these articles in two piles: "protected" and "threatened." Each group should be prepared to explain briefly why the article was chosen for the pile. If you like, you can turn this activity into a competition for the most articles.

Call to Family, Community, and Participation

Divide the class into small groups. Give each small group a poster board with two large concentric circles drawn on it. Also give them piles of magazines. In the inner circle, have them make a collage of families (showing how they come in many different sizes and shapes). In the outer circle, have them make a collage depicting the institutions that support the common good—the good of all people (for example, schools, companies, media, and government). Each group should present its collage and describe how Catholics can act to strengthen families and to build a society in which the dignity of all people is respected.

Rights and Responsibilities

Divide the class into small groups. Ask each group to come up with a children's "bill of rights." Each list of rights should begin with the phrase, "All children have a right to . . ." After each group comes up with a list of rights, compare it to the rights named in Catholic social teaching. See the essay on "Rights and Responsibilities" on page 60 for background material. Did the students miss any? Ask them how their lists of rights might differ if they were living in poverty? What rights would rise to the top of the list in that situation? What "rights" would be nice but are "extras"? Ask them to revise their lists and to put a "B" next to those "rights" that are "basic" and an "X" next to those "rights" that are just "nice extras." To prepare for this session, you might want to learn about the United Nations Convention on the Rights of the Child. Go online to *www.unicef.org/crc//crc.htm* for more information. The Holy See (the Vatican) has ratified this convention; the United States is one of only two nations that have not. You could add a "justice project" to the conclusion of the class and ask your students to write their senators in the U.S. Congress and the President, asking them to ratify the United Nations Convention on the Rights of the Child.

Option for and with the Poor and Vulnerable

Visit the Poverty USA website of the Catholic Campaign for Human Development at *www.usccb.org/cchd/povertyusa*. Take the "tour" of poverty and then design your own in-class poverty budget exercise. Have your students start with income from a poverty-wage job (that is, minimum wage) and then subtract average expenses for shelter, food, transportation, clothing, medical care, and other essentials. Your students will be amazed at how quickly they run out of money. Discuss the struggles of working poor families. Use the fact sheets from the website to enhance your discussion.

Dignity of Work and the Rights of Workers

A good way to get young people interested in the rights of workers is to have them take a look at the issues of child labor and sweatshops. The Archdiocese of Newark (NJ) has developed a program on sweatshops. Go online to *www.rcan.org/humanconcerns/ sweatshoptruefalse.htm/*, and use the quiz to raise awareness about sweatshops. Or call the archdiocese's Human Concerns Office to order a full set of materials on Catholic teaching and sweatshops. Young people also can become involved in Catholic Relief Service's Fair Trade Coffee program, through which workers are ensured fair wages. Go online to *www.catholicrelief.org/fairtrade/coffee* for more information.

Solidarity

Do some research on the per-capita income of the United States and two or three nations in the developing world. Calculate a ratio that represents the relative income of each country in relation to the United States. Using small, bite-sized candies, prepare bags of candy with the same ratio of candies: one bag for the United States, and one for each of the other nations. Divide the class into the same number of groups as you have nations. Give each group an information sheet on its nation that includes per-capita income and other facts. Ask the group to prepare a brief presentation of the information to the class by pretending it is from the country and is talking about its situation. After the presentations, give each group its bag of candy. Discuss the groups' reactions to receiving different amounts. Connect this fact to the reality of inequality in the world.

Care for God's Creation

Divide the class into an even number of groups. Give each group poster board and plenty of magazines. Ask half the groups to make collages that depict the beauty and interdependence of God's creation. "Interdependence" means how the health of nature and creatures are intertwined. Ask the other groups to make collages that depict how humanity is harming God's creation. Ask each group to make a brief presentation of their collage. A follow-up service project might involve recycling or outdoor clean-up at a park or along a waterway. Be sure to get parental permission slips for off-site projects.

SUMMARIZE *3 minutes*

Use the background material in the "Essay" on the theme to summarize the Church's teaching and to make connections to the above exercise.

CLOSING PRAYER AND REFLECTIONS *5 minutes*

Acknowledge that the teachings of Jesus challenge each of us individually and society as a whole. Remind the class that Jesus calls us to be the "light of the world" (Mt 5:14) and to spread the light of his teachings. Invite each participant to share a brief phrase that comes to mind in response to the question, How is God calling you to walk in the footsteps of Jesus and be a light in the world? Pause for reflection and invite students to share their phrases without elaboration or discussion. Note that we pray for the coming of God's Kingdom and for God's will to be done on earth each time we pray the Lord's Prayer. Lead the group in closing with the Our Father.

Sample Sessions
and Outlines

for Grades 10-12

Session One

Anchoring Catholic Social Teaching in the Footsteps of Jesus

TOTAL TIME: 1 HOUR

PREPARATION

Read over this sample outline, the summary of Part I of the video on page 1, and the essay "Overview of Catholic Social Teaching" on pages 50-52. Preview Part I of the video *In the Footsteps of Jesus: Catholic Social Teaching at Work Today*. Make available Bibles, pencils or pens, and paper for your students. Place an open Bible at the front of the classroom in a place of honor, perhaps propped on a cloth matching the color of the Church's liturgical season and between candles (if the fire code permits). Decide ahead of time on a simple and quick way to divide the class into small groups of four to six persons. You might use color-coded nametags for this purpose. Write the small-group discussion questions from the outline on a board or flip chart. Place and test the television/video player and set the video to the start of the tape. Select a reader and leader for prayer.

OPENING PRAYER
4 minutes

Welcome your students. Give any instructions related to the prayer time. Ask them to place themselves in the presence of the Lord. See "Prayer for the Light of the World" on page 9.

INTRODUCTION
5 minutes

Tell your students that today's lesson is about Jesus and his call to transform our world. Ask these or similar questions:

1. Which of the teachings of Jesus would help us to build a better world?
2. Which of these teachings of Jesus do you find difficult to put into practice?

Encourage your students to share brief answers to these questions out loud with the class. Thank the more vocal students for their answers, and then ask for anyone who has not spoken to add reflections. Depending on the nature of the group, you might even call upon quieter students by name.

INTRODUCE THE VIDEO *1 minute*

Use the brief description on page 1 of the resource manual to introduce Part I of the video *In the Footsteps of Jesus*. Ask the students to look for examples of the teaching of Jesus in the video and of how the Church has applied this teaching to our world today.

VIEW PART I OF THE VIDEO *9 minutes*

DEBRIEF/REVIEW THE VIDEO *7 minutes*

Use the following questions to help your students recall some of the major points covered by the video. Simply present the questions to the whole group, asking them to keep their responses brief. (This is not a time for discussion; the goal is to review briefly the content of the video.) Give quieter members of the class an opportunity to contribute. Affirm vocal individuals, and then gently redirect your attention to allow other students to join in.

Questions for Reviewing Part I of the Video
1. What teachings of Jesus are mentioned in the video?
2. Which of today's social issues are mentioned in the video?
3. Which key themes of Catholic social teaching can you remember?

SMALL-GROUP DISCUSSION: EXPLORING THE TEACHING OF JESUS
15 minutes

The purpose of these small-group discussions is to have students grapple with challenging teachings of Jesus that have implications for social issues today. Be careful not to give the impression that Jesus gives simple answers to today's complex social questions. Instead show that the teachings of Jesus suggest values that guide the Church's teaching on today's issues.

Divide the class into several groups. Give every member of the class a Bible (or at least one per group). Assign one of the following passages from the Gospels to each group:

Matthew 5:1-16
Matthew 5:38-48
Matthew 25:31-46
Mark 12:28-34
Luke 4:16-21
Luke 6:17-26
Luke 6:27-38

Invite each group to read its assigned passage from the Gospels and discuss the following questions (which are written on the board or flip chart). Remind groups of how much time they will have, and ask them to select a person to briefly summarize their answers to these questions:

1. How would our world be different if people put this teaching into practice?
2. What suffering in today's world might be eased if more people followed this teaching of Jesus?

LARGE-GROUP FEEDBACK *8 minutes*

Invite an individual in each group to summarize briefly its answers to the above questions. Draw parallels between key insights that are shared by different groups, and invite students to add insights or to ask questions. Affirm the participation of the more vocal members of the class, but redirect attention to others through invitations and open-ended questions.

DEBRIEF *5 minutes*

Acknowledge that the teachings of Jesus challenge each of us individually and society as a whole. Remind students that Jesus calls us to be the "light of the world" (Mt 5:14) and to spread the light of his teachings. Invite each student to select one teaching that he or she believes our world needs to put into practice at this time. Have each of them share why they selected the teaching with the others in the small group.

CLOSING PRAYER
2 minutes

Remind your students that they are called to be the "light of the world" (Mt 5:14) and to spread the light of Jesus' teachings. Note that we pray for the coming of God's Kingdom and for God's will to be done on earth each time we pray the Lord's Prayer. Lead the class in closing with the Our Father.

ALTERNATIVE ACTIVITY

Use the "What Did Jesus Teach?" exercise that starts on page 80.

Session Two
Exploring the Themes of Catholic Social Teaching

TOTAL TIME: 1 HOUR

PREPARATION

Read over this sample outline, the summary of Part II of the video on page 2, and the section of this resource manual on "Seven Themes of Catholic Social Teaching" that starts on page 53. Preview Part II of the video *In the Footsteps of Jesus: Catholic Social Teaching at Work Today*. Make copies of the essay "Seven Themes of Catholic Social Teaching" on pages 53-54 for each member of the class. Place an open Bible at the front of the classroom in a place of honor, perhaps propped on a cloth matching the color of the Church's liturgical season and between candles (if the fire code permits). Place and test the television/video player; set the video to the start of Part II of the tape. (Advance the tape to 10:36 minutes.) Select a reader and leader for prayer.

OPENING PRAYER

4 minutes

Welcome your students. Give any instructions related to the prayer time. Ask them to place themselves in the presence of the Lord. See "Prayer for God's Spirit of Justice" on page 10.

INTRODUCTION

5 minutes

Tell your students that today's lesson will focus on the seven themes of Catholic social teaching. The Church has identified these themes based on the teaching of Jesus, the foundation of the Scriptures, and the aid of the Holy Spirit. Ask these or similar questions:

1. What do you know about Catholic social teaching?
2. Can you remember any of the basic themes of Catholic social teaching from Part I of the video (the last session)?

Encourage your students to share brief answers to these questions out loud with the class. Thank the more vocal students for their answers, and then ask for anyone who has not spoken to add reflections. Depending on the nature of the group, you might even call upon quieter students by name.

INTRODUCE THE VIDEO *1 minute*

Use the summary on page 2 of Part II of the video *In the Footsteps of Jesus*. Ask the students to pay particular attention to the seven themes of Catholic social teaching. See if they can remember them all at the end of the video.

VIEW PART II OF THE VIDEO *19 minutes*

DEBRIEF/REVIEW THE VIDEO *7 minutes*

Use the following questions to help your students recall some of the major points covered by the video. Ask them to keep their responses brief. (This is not a time for discussion; the goal is to review briefly the content of the video.) Give quieter members of the class an opportunity to contribute. Affirm vocal individuals, and then gently redirect your attention to allow other students to join in.

Questions for Reviewing Part II of the Video

1. The video included seven testimonies by individuals and a couple who have lived Catholic social teaching. Which testimony did you find particularly moving? Why?
2. Which key themes of Catholic social teaching can you remember? (Consider writing them on the board or a flip chart as each is identified. See how many the class can come up with. Affirm their successes!)

SEVEN THEMES OF CATHOLIC SOCIAL TEACHING

15 minutes

The life and teaching of Jesus is the foundation of the Church's social teaching, but over the centuries the Church, inspired by the Holy Spirit, has developed a body of social teaching that guides Catholics as we work to build a better world. The Catholic bishops of the United States have identified seven key themes of Catholic social teaching.

Pass out copies of "Seven Themes of Catholic Social Teaching." Use the above information to introduce this topic to your students. Divide the class into small groups of three to six individuals each. Assign each group one or two themes. Ask each small group to read the theme(s) and then to come up with a list of today's social issues for which this theme has implications. Ask them to simply name the issues, not to resolve what should be done for each issue. Explain that the goal is to identify some of the social implications of the theme. For example, the seventh theme has implications for laws that encourage recycling. Ask each small group to be prepared to do the following with the large group: (1) Select someone to read the theme(s) to the large group; and (2) select someone else to list five or more of today's social issues for which this theme has implications. Remind them of how much time they will have.

REPORTS FROM SMALL GROUPS *10 minutes*

Invite each small group to give a one-minute report on each theme. Simply read the theme to the group. Then briefly list five or more contemporary social issues related to the theme.

CLOSING PRAYER

2 minutes

Remind your students that they are given the gift of the Holy Spirit to help them transform the world by putting the themes of Catholic social teaching into practice. Note that we pray for the coming of God's Kingdom and for God's will to be done on earth each time we pray the Lord's Prayer. Lead the class in closing with the Our Father.

ALTERNATIVE ACTIVITY

Give students the "Catholic Social Teaching Multiple Choice Quiz" on page 90.

Session Three
Walking in the Footsteps of Jesus

TOTAL TIME: 1 HOUR

PREPARATION

Read over this outline and "Walking in the Footsteps of Jesus" on pages 70-73. Preview the last segment of Part II of the video, *In the Footsteps of Jesus: Catholic Social Teaching at Work Today*, beginning at 25:00 minutes. Contact your parish's social ministry committee to identify potential service or justice projects for your class to consider. Have a number of both types of projects for them to discuss. (Note: Over time, it is important to give your students experiences with both types of responses to Catholic social teaching.) Place and test the television/video player; set the video at the start of the last segment of the tape after the seventh theme in Part II. (Advance the tape to 25:00 minutes.) Have a board or flip chart ready for use. Select a reader and leader for prayer.

OPENING PRAYER

4 minutes

Welcome your students. Give any instructions related to the prayer time. Ask them to place themselves in the presence of the Lord. See "Prayer for Light in the Darkness" on page 11.

INTRODUCTION

5 minutes

Tell your students that today's lesson is about responding to Catholic social teaching and walking in the footsteps of Jesus. Ask these or similar questions:

1. Many of the teachings of Jesus would help us to build a better world. What are some of the teachings of Jesus that we looked at in past sessions?
2. The Holy Spirit has inspired the Church to build upon the foundation of Jesus' teachings and to develop Catholic social teaching. What are the major themes of Catholic social teaching?

Encourage your students to share brief answers to these questions out loud with the class. Thank the more vocal students for their answers, and then ask for anyone who has not spoken to add reflections. Depending on the nature of the group, you might even call upon quieter students by name.

INTRODUCE THE VIDEO *1 minute*

Tell the class that they have already seen Part II of the video *In the Footsteps of Jesus*. Indicate that you are going to show them only the final segment of the video that suggests ways that we can put into practice the themes of Catholic social teaching.

VIEW THE FINAL SEGMENT OF PART II OF THE VIDEO

DEBRIEF/REVIEW THE VIDEO *5 minutes*

Use the following questions to help your students recall some of the major points covered by the video. Ask them to keep their responses brief. (This is not a time for discussion; the goal is to review briefly the content of the video.) Give quieter members of the class an opportunity to contribute. Affirm vocal individuals, and then gently redirect your attention to allow other students to join in.

Questions for Reviewing the Final Segment of Part II of the Video
1. When asked what to do to make a difference in the world, what advice did Blessed Teresa of Calcutta offer? ("Just do what's in front of you.") What did she mean? What is in front of us?
2. The video mentioned a number of ways to put Catholic social teaching into practice. What were some of the ways that the video mentioned?

CHARITY AND JUSTICE
10 minutes

Use the "Charity and Justice" section on page 70 to explain the basic distinction to your students. The following chart may help.

Charity:	Justice:
Focuses on the needs of people	Focuses on the rights of people
Looks at individual situations	Analyzes social situations or structures
Meets immediate needs	Works for long-term social change
Addresses painful symptoms of social problems	Addresses underlying social causes
Relies on the generosity of donors	Relies on just laws and fair social structures

Next draw a vertical line down the center of the board or flip chart. Title the left side "Charity" and the right side "Justice." Ask your students to list ways to put Catholic social teaching into practice. (Hint: They can draw upon the examples from the video.) Place examples of charity in the left column and examples of justice in the right column.

SERVICE AND JUSTICE PROJECTS *20 minutes*

Describe service projects and justice projects recommended by your parish's social ministry committee. As you describe each project, ask students to identify if it is a service (charity) or justice (social change) project. List the projects on the board in columns similar to the ones used in the last exercise.

Help your students to discuss the pluses and minuses of each project. Following are some criteria to consider:

- Does Catholic social teaching call upon them to address the need or injustice?
- Does the group have access to the gifts, talents, and resources required for the project?
- Does the project address a basic human need or correct a basic injustice with which the students are familiar (or with which they can become familiar)? (Remember Blessed Teresa of Calcutta's advice: "Do what's in front of you"?)
- Does the group have partners in the wider Church or community with whom they can work on the project?

Make sure each possible project is within the capability of your students. You will need to secure parental permission for projects off-site. Over time, try to engage your students in both service and justice projects. For example, one time they might serve a meal in a soup kitchen or collect food for low-income families—a charitable service project. The next time they might write to members of the U.S. Congress about world hunger and foreign aid—a justice project.

PLANNING *11 minutes*

If time permits, get the students involved in planning how they will do the project. You might want to have someone from the parish's social ministry committee join the class during their next meeting. The more the youth are involved in planning, the more committed they will be to the project. This involvement also builds leadership skills and models Catholic social teaching in action. Affirm their plans. It is also a good idea to debrief the students after they undertake the project—helping them to reflect on it in prayer and in light of Catholic social teaching.

CLOSING PRAYER
10 minutes

Remind your students that they are called to be the "light of the world" (Mt 5:14) and to spread the light of Catholic social teaching. Note that we pray for the coming of God's Kingdom and for God's will to be done on earth each time we pray the Lord's Prayer. Lead them in the Lord's Prayer.

**OPTIONAL OR
ALTERNATIVE ACTIVITY**

OPTIONAL OR ALTERNATIVE ACTIVITY
Use the "Stand Up If . . ." exercise on pages 92-95.

Additional Sessions for Grades 10-12

See the suggestions for grades 7-9 on pages 20-27 and for young adults and adults on pages 38-46. Depending upon the makeup of your group, many of the suggestions for grades 7-9 can be adapted for use with older students. Also, many senior high groups can use the adult education model successfully.

Sample Sessions
and Outlines

for Young Adults and Adults

There are many opportunities in parish life for adults to explore the seven themes of Catholic social teaching. Such exploration can take place in adult education programs, in sacramental preparation programs for parents, and in sessions with catechumens and candidates for reception into the Church. It can also take place in meetings of small faith-sharing groups, young adult gatherings, men's and women's groups, parish committees, and parish councils. It is particularly appropriate to incorporate study of Catholic social teaching in training sessions for catechists.

In sessions with adults, especially in smaller group settings, special care must be taken to respect the nature of adult learning. Adults bring a lot of life experience to the learning process. Although didactic presentations have their place in conveying basic knowledge and information—for example, surveying the history or content of papal and episcopal Catholic social teaching documents—it is also important for adults to grapple with the basic themes of Catholic social teaching in discussion-oriented settings in which a skilled facilitator guides the group. The facilitator is not a teacher, but rather a "co-learner" who supports and orients the group discussion. See "Help for Group Facilitators and Leaders" on pages 74-77 for more information on this important role.

The facilitator will also want to review the section "Avoiding Ideological Conflicts" on page 76. It may be helpful to set basic ground rules for group discussions, especially in Session Three, where the focus moves from the themes of Catholic social teaching to their application to social issues and projects.

Session One
Anchoring Catholic Social Teaching in the Footsteps of Jesus

TOTAL TIME: 75 MINUTES

PREPARATION	Read over this sample outline, the summary of Part I of the video on page 1, and the essay "Overview of Catholic Social Teaching" on pages 50-52. Preview Part I of the video *In the Footsteps of Jesus: Catholic Social Teaching at Work Today*. Have Bibles, paper, and pens or pencils available for all the members of the group. Place an open Bible at the front of the room in a place of honor, perhaps propped on a cloth matching the color of the Church's liturgical season and between candles (if the fire code permits). Have nametags available for people to put on as they arrive. Arrange seating in the room so that the members of the group face one another. Place and test the television/video player and set the video to the start of the tape. Select a reader and leader for prayer.
OPTIONAL OR ALTERNATIVE ACTIVITY	To deepen the group's preparation for the session, give them copies of the essay "Overview of Catholic Social Teaching" to read before the meeting.
OPENING PRAYER *4 minutes*	Welcome the participants. Give any instructions related to the prayer time. Ask them to place themselves in the presence of the Lord. See "Prayer for the Light of the World" on page 9.
INTRODUCTION *5 minutes*	Tell your group that today's session is about Jesus and his call to transform our world. Ask these or similar questions:

1. Which of the teachings of Jesus would help us to build a better world?
2. Which of these teachings of Jesus do you find difficult to put into practice?

Encourage the group to share brief answers to these questions. Thank the more vocal participants for their answers, and then ask for anyone who has not spoken to add reflections. Depending on the nature of the group, you might even call upon quieter members by name.

INTRODUCE THE VIDEO *1 minute*	Use the brief description on page 1 to introduce Part I of the video *In the Footsteps of Jesus*. Ask the participants to look for examples of the teaching of Jesus in the video and how the Church has applied this teaching to our world today.
VIEW PART I OF THE VIDEO *9 minutes*	
DEBRIEF/REVIEW THE VIDEO *13 minutes*	Use the following questions to help the participants recall some of the major points covered by the video. Ask them to keep their responses brief. (This is not a time for discussion; the goal is to review briefly the content of the video.) Give quieter members of the group an opportunity to contribute. Affirm vocal individuals, and then gently redirect your attention to allow other participants to join in.

Questions for Reviewing Part I of the Video
1. What teachings of Jesus are mentioned in the video?
2. Which of today's social issues are mentioned in the video?
3. Which key themes of Catholic social teaching can you remember?

GROUP DISCUSSION: EXPLORING THE TEACHING OF JESUS
35 minutes

The purpose of this small-group discussion is to have the participants grapple with teachings of Jesus that have implications for social issues today. Be careful not to give the impression that Jesus gives simple answers to today's complex social questions. Instead mention that the teachings of Jesus suggest values that guide the Church's teaching on contemporary issues.

Invite a member of the group to read slowly Matthew 5:1-16 while the others follow along with their Bibles. At the conclusion of the reading, ask the participants to take a few moments to quietly reflect on the following question:

In this passage, what word, phrase, or image did you find particularly moving or challenging?

After a short pause, invite the members of the group to simply share the word, phrase, or image without explanation or comment. (This initial round of sharing is not meant to be a discussion; it is meant to be more reflective.) It might be good for the facilitator to model a brief response before inviting others to share. Be sure everyone has a chance to name a word, phrase, or image. Of course, it is okay for someone to pass.

Now use the following discussion questions to explore the social implications of this teaching:

1. When you think about our world today, what about this teaching makes you comfortable or uncomfortable?
2. In what ways does this teaching affirm aspects of our society's laws, economic practices, or cultural values?
3. In what ways does this teaching challenge aspects of our society's laws, economic practices, or cultural values?

The final question focuses on the implications of this passage for the members of the group in their social roles and responsibilities. Read and reread this question slowly so that participants have time to consider one or another of their social roles in relation to the passage.

4. What does this teaching challenge you to do in your role as a family member, worker, owner, investor, consumer, or citizen?

OTHER OPTIONS

The above discussion process can be used with other biblical passages that present teachings of Jesus that have profound social implications. Suggested Scriptures are Matthew 5:38-48, Matthew 25:31-46, Mark 12:28-34, Luke 4:16-21, Luke 6:17-26, and Luke 6:27-38. If your group is open to games, you might even use the "What Did Jesus Teach?" exercise that is described on page 80.

CLOSING PRAYER AND REFLECTIONS *5 minutes*

Acknowledge that the teachings of Jesus challenge each of us individually and society as a whole. Remind the group that Jesus calls us to be the "light of the world" (Mt 5:14) and to spread the light of his teachings. Invite each participant to share one word, image, or phrase that captures a key insight that they gained during this session. Pause for reflection, and invite participants to share their words, images, or phrases without elaboration or discussion. Note that we pray for the coming of God's Kingdom and for God's will to be done on earth each time we pray the Lord's Prayer. Lead the group in closing with the Our Father.

Session Two
Exploring the Themes of Catholic Social Teaching

PREPARATION

Read over this sample outline, the summary of Part II of the video *In the Footsteps of Jesus: Catholic Social Teaching at Work Today* on page 2, and the essay "Seven Themes of Catholic Social Teaching" on pages 53-54. Preview Part II of the video. Make copies of "Seven Themes of Catholic Social Teaching" for each member of the group. Place an open Bible in a place of honor, perhaps propped on a cloth matching the color of the Church's liturgical season and between candles (if the fire code permits). Place and test the television/video player, and set the video to the start of Part II of the tape. (Advance the tape to 10:36 minutes.) Select a reader and leader for prayer.

OPTIONAL OR ALTERNATIVE ACTIVITY

Prior to the session, pass out copies of "Seven Themes of Catholic Social Teaching" on pages 53-54 for participants to read.

OPENING PRAYER
4 minutes

Welcome the participants. Give any instructions related to the prayer time. Ask them to place themselves in the presence of the Lord. See "Prayer for God's Spirit of Justice" on page 10.

INTRODUCTION
5 minutes

Tell your group that today's session will focus on the seven themes of Catholic social teaching. The Church has identified these themes based on the teaching of Jesus and the foundation of the Scriptures, with the aid of the Holy Spirit. Ask these or similar questions:

1. What social issues has the Church addressed publicly in recent years?
2. What basic themes or values lie behind the Church's positions on social issues?

Encourage the participants to share brief answers to these questions. (This is a time for simply naming issues and values, not for discussing them.) Thank the more vocal members of the group for their answers, and then ask for anyone who has not spoken to add reflections. Depending on the nature of the group, you might even call upon quieter members by name.

INTRODUCE THE VIDEO *1 minute*

Use the summary of Part II of the video *In the Footsteps of Jesus*. Ask the participants to pay particular attention to the seven themes of Catholic social teaching.

VIEW PART II OF THE VIDEO *19 minutes*

Use the following questions to help your group recall some of the major points covered by the video. Ask the group to keep their responses brief. (This is not a time for discussion; the goal is to review briefly the content of the video.) Give quieter members of the class an opportunity to contribute. Affirm vocal individuals, and then gently redirect your attention to allow others to join in.

Questions for Reviewing Part II of the Video
1. The video includes seven testimonies by individuals and a couple who have lived out Catholic social teaching. Which testimony did you find particularly moving? Why?
2. Which of the seven themes, if any, do you find surprising or confusing?

The life and teaching of Jesus is the foundation of the Church's social teaching, but over the centuries the Church, inspired by the Holy Spirit, has developed a body of social teaching that guides us as we work for a better world. The Catholic bishops of the United States have identified seven key themes of Catholic social teaching.

Make sure participants have copies of "Seven Themes of Catholic Social Teaching" from page 53. (Be sure to have extra copies on hand in case someone forgets to bring theirs.) Use the above information to introduce this topic to the group. Taking each theme in order, use the following process for each:

1. Ask a participant to read the theme to the group as the others follow along on their sheets. (Alternate this responsibility among group members.)

2. Invite the participants to ask clarifying questions about the theme. As these questions are asked, invite the members of the group to share responses. Resist becoming the "answer person."

3. Discussion question: When you reflect on this theme, what social issues in our community, nation, or world come to mind? Why?

NOTE: This discussion is not a time to debate the relative merits of various solutions to complex social problems. Instead this discussion is meant to identify issues, showing the relevance of the themes for the social challenges that we face today. Keep the discussion moving. Remember that you have seven themes to explore in the time allotted for you discussion.

Remind your group that each of us is given the gift of the Holy Spirit to help us transform the world by putting the themes of Catholic social teaching into practice. Note that we pray for the coming of God's Kingdom and for God's will to be done on earth each time we pray the Lord's Prayer. Lead the class in closing with the Our Father.

Session Three
Walking in the Footsteps of Jesus

TOTAL TIME: 75 MINUTES

PREPARATION

Read over "Walking in the Footsteps of Jesus" and its section on "Charity and Justice" on pages 70-72. Preview the last segment of Part II of the video *In the Footsteps of Jesus: Catholic Social Teaching at Work Today* (beginning at 25:00 minutes). Contact your parish's social ministry committee to identify potential service or justice projects for your group to consider. (Note: Over time, it is important to give your group experiences with both types of responses to Catholic social teaching.) Place and test the television/video player; set the video to the start at the last segment of the tape after the seventh theme in Part II. (Advance the video to 25:00 minutes.) Select a reader and leader for prayer.

OPTIONAL OR ALTERNATIVE ACTIVITY

Prior to the session, give participants copies of "Walking in the Footsteps of Jesus" and "Charity and Justice" on pages 70-72 to read.

OPENING PRAYER
4 minutes

Welcome the participants. Give any instructions related to the prayer time. Ask them to place themselves in the presence of the Lord. See "Prayer for Light in the Darkness" on page 11.

INTRODUCTION
5 minutes

Tell the participants that today's session is about responding to Catholic social teaching and walking in the footsteps of Jesus. Based on the groups' prior discussions of the video *In the Footsteps of Jesus*, how would they answer these (or similar) questions:

1. What key values guide the Church's engagement with social issues today?
2. What are some of the social issues that face our community, nation, and world?

Encourage participants to share brief answers to these questions with the group. Thank the more vocal participants for their answers, and then ask for anyone who has not spoken to add reflections. Depending on the nature of the group, you might even call upon quieter participants by name.

INTRODUCE THE VIDEO *1 minute*

Remind the group that they have already seen Part II of the video *In the Footsteps of Jesus*. Indicate that you are just going to show them the final segment of the video that suggests ways that we can put into practice the themes of Catholic social teaching.

VIEW THE FINAL SEGMENT OF PART II OF THE VIDEO *2.5 minutes*

DEBRIEF/REVIEW THE VIDEO *8 minutes*

Use the following questions to help participants recall some of the major points covered by the video. Ask them to keep their responses brief. (This is not a time for discussion; the goal is to review briefly the content of the video.) Give quieter members of the class an opportunity to contribute. Affirm vocal individuals, and then gently redirect your attention to allow other students to join in.

Questions for Reviewing the Final Segment of Part II of the Video
1. When asked what to do to make a difference in the world, Blessed Teresa of Calcutta said, "Just do what's in front of you." What is in front of us in our local community? In our nation? In our world?
2. The video mentions a number of ways to put Catholic social teaching into practice. What were some of them?

CHARITY AND JUSTICE
10 minutes

Make sure participants have copies of "Charity and Justice" from pages 70-72. (Have extra copies on hand for those who may have forgotten to bring theirs.) Give them a couple of minutes to read or reacquaint themselves with the material. Then briefly discuss these questions:

1. How are charity and justice distinct?
2. Why are charity and justice incomplete without one another?
3. Are you more comfortable with working for charity or for justice? Why?

WHERE IS YOUR FAITH CALLING YOU TO HELP? *38 minutes*

Give the participants some quiet time to reflect on the following questions:

1. What is in front of you? Where is your faith calling you to help?
2. What gifts and talents do you have to share with others?
3. How is God calling you to follow in the footsteps of Jesus to put his teaching into practice in the world? Try to identify at least one act of charity and one work of justice that God has put in front of you.

Next lead participants in a discussion of the above questions. Keep the group's sharing personal and reflective. (This is a time for sharing hopes and struggles, not a time for debating the relative merits of each other's ideas.) Make sure everyone is able to identify at least one act of charity and one work of justice to consider. These "footsteps" need not be giant steps; they could be as modest as making a contribution to a local organization that does good work or writing a public official about an issue of social concern.

SERVICE OR JUSTICE PROJECT *2 minutes*

Describe a possible service project or justice project that is recommended by your parish's social ministry committee. Give members of the group information on how to get involved. If the group is ongoing, try to offer its members opportunities to participate in both service and justice projects. For example, one time they might serve a meal in a soup kitchen or collect food for low-income families. This would be a charitable service project. The next time they might write to members of the U.S. Congress about world hunger and foreign aid. This would be a justice project.

CLOSING PRAYER
2 minutes

Remind participants that as Christians they are called to be the "light of the world" (Mt 5:14) and to spread the light of Catholic social teaching. Note that we pray for the coming of God's Kingdom and for God's will to be done on earth each time we pray the Lord's Prayer. Lead them in the Lord's Prayer.

Outline
for Additional Sessions for Young Adults and Adults

TOTAL TIME: 75 MINUTES

INTRODUCTION

More in-depth sessions on each of the seven themes of Catholic social teaching can be designed using the following generic outline.

PREPARATION

Prior to the session, give participants copies of the essay on the theme to read. Ask them to underline any sections that they think are particularly important. Have them place question marks next to any concepts that are unclear to them. Make copies of the theme's corresponding "Scripture and Tradition" sheet for use during the session. (See pages 55-69 for the theme-related essays and "Scripture and Tradition" sheets.) Preview the segment of Part II of the video *In the Footsteps of Jesus: Catholic Social Teaching at Work Today* related to the theme. The time segments are as follows:

Advance tape to:	Theme:
11:35 minutes	Life and Dignity of the Human Person
14:42 minutes	Call to Family, Community, and Participation
16:45 minutes	Rights and Responsibilities
18:02 minutes	Option for and with the Poor and Vulnerable
19:45 minutes	Dignity of Work and the Rights of Workers
21:40 minutes	Solidarity
23:16 minutes	Care for God's Creation

Place and test the television/video player; set the video to start at the beginning of the appropriate segment.

PRAYER *3 minutes*

Open with a short prayer based on the theme using the "Prayer Service on the Seven Themes of Catholic Social Teaching: Our Call, Our Tradition " on pages 12-14.

INTRODUCE THE VIDEO *1 minute*

Use the brief description of the theme to introduce the segment of Part II of the video *In the Footsteps of Jesus*.

VIEW THE THEME'S SEGMENT ON PART II OF THE VIDEO *2.5 minutes*

DEBRIEF/REVIEW THE VIDEO *8 minutes*

Use the following questions to help participants recall some of the major points covered by the video. Ask them to keep their responses brief. (This is not a time for discussion; the goal is to review briefly the content of the video.) Give quieter members of the group an opportunity to contribute. Affirm vocal individuals, and then gently redirect your attention to allow other participants to join in.

Questions for Reviewing the Video Segment
1. What image or insight from the video segment caught your attention?
2. What implication of this theme is especially countercultural today?

GROUP DISCUSSION: EXPLORING THE THEME

The purpose of this small-group discussion is to have the participants grapple with the theme in Scripture and Catholic Tradition.

CLARIFY THE THEME
5 minutes

Before beginning this discussion, ask if anyone has questions about the reading that they did on the theme prior to the session. Invite participants to respond to questions that are raised.

REFLECT ON SCRIPTURE
20 minutes

Pass out copies of the "Scripture and Tradition" sheet related to the theme. Invite a member of the group to read the Scripture from the "Scripture and Tradition" sheet. At the conclusion of the reading, ask the participants to take a few quiet moments to reflect on the following question:

1. In this passage, what word, phrase, or image did you find particularly moving or challenging?

After a short pause, invite the members of the group to share the word, phrase, or image without explanation or comment. (This initial round of sharing is not meant to be a discussion; it is meant to be more reflective.) It might be good for the facilitator to model a brief response before inviting others to share. Be sure that everyone has a chance to name a word, phrase, or image. Of course, it is always okay for someone to pass.

Next invite group members to discuss the social implications of the Scripture with this question:

2. How does this Scripture affirm or challenge our society or world?

REFLECT ON TRADITION *30 minutes*

Ask someone else to read aloud the quotations from Catholic social teaching from the "Catholic Social Teaching" section of the sheet. Use the following discussion questions to explore the social implications of this teaching:

1. When you think about our world today, what (if anything) about this teaching makes you comfortable or uncomfortable?
2. In what ways does this teaching affirm aspects of our society's laws, economic practices, and cultural values?
3. In what ways does this teaching challenge aspects of our society's laws, economic practices, and cultural values?

The final question focuses on the implications of the passage for the members of the group in their social roles and responsibilities. Read and reread this question slowly so that participants have time to consider one or another of their social roles in relation to the passage.

4. What does this teaching challenge you to do in your role as a family member, worker, owner, investor, consumer, or citizen?

CLOSING PRAYER AND REFLECTION *5 minutes*

Acknowledge that the teachings of Jesus challenge each of us individually and society as a whole. Remind the group that Jesus calls us to be the "light of the world" (Mt 5:14) and to spread the light of his teachings. Invite each participant to share one word or a brief phrase that comes to mind in response to the question, How is God calling you to follow in the footsteps of Jesus and put his teaching into practice in the world? Pause for reflection and invite participants to share their word, image, or phrase without elaboration or discussion. Note that we pray for the coming of God's Kingdom and for God's will to be done on earth each time we pray the Lord's Prayer. Lead the group in closing with the Our Father.

Essays
and Handouts on

Catholic Social
Teaching

Overview
of Catholic Social Teaching

Catholic social teaching finds its beginning and end in the person of Jesus. Jesus is the Christ, the *alpha* and the *omega*, the beginning and the end (Rev 1:8). In the life and death of Jesus of Nazareth, we find God's presence embodied in human history. In the mission and teaching of Jesus, we find revealed God's plan for each of us individually, for humanity, and indeed for all creation, as a whole (Rom 8).

In the Gospel of Luke, Jesus begins his public ministry by applying these words of the prophet Isaiah to his own life and mission:

"The Spirit of the Lord is upon me, / because he has anointed me / to bring glad tidings to the poor. / He has sent me to proclaim liberty to captives / and recovery of sight to the blind, / to let the oppressed go free, / and to proclaim a year acceptable to the Lord." (Lk 4:18-19)

Jesus' teaching and example have implications for both our personal lives and the society in which we live. While not in any way minimizing the call of the Gospel for us to transform our personal lives, this study of the seven themes of Catholic social teaching will focus on the transformation of our society—a transformation that begins with our transformed hearts and minds.

These early years of the third millennium are an appropriate time to deepen our grasp of Catholic social teaching and to strengthen our work for the Church's social mission. Pope John Paul II called us to this renewed commitment in the Great Jubilee Year 2000. Our Holy Father reminded us that the social mission of the Church finds its roots in the jubilee traditions of liberty—letting land lie fallow, freeing slaves, relieving debts, and letting the oppressed go free (cf. Lv 25).

Catholic social teaching is not new; it is as ancient as the Scriptures. Yet Catholic social teaching is ever new; it is a living tradition that has grown throughout the centuries as God's people have encountered new social realities and challenges. Catholic social teaching is like an ancient oak tree. Its

roots are the Scriptures that firmly anchor it. Its trunk has grown in girth throughout the centuries, especially in the last 110 years as the Church has confronted the rapidly changing social realities of the industrial revolution and modern life. Its branches reach toward the sky of tomorrow, drawing energy from the sun of God's Reign of justice and peace.

Catholic social teaching is a living tradition rooted in the soil of human experience and shaped by the climate of changing social realities. Just as the growth of a tree responds to the conditions of soil, rainfall, and climate, Catholic social teaching takes shape in response to the human condition but draws energy and inspiration from the eternal Word of God.

In the words of the *Catechism of the Catholic Church* (Washington, DC: Liberia Editrice Vaticana–USCCB, 2000, 2nd ed.), "The Church's social teaching comprises a body of doctrine, which is articulated as the Church interprets events in the course of history, with the assistance of the Holy Spirit, in the light of the whole of what has been revealed by Jesus Christ" (no. 2422). The *Catechism* also states, "The development of the doctrine of the Church on economic and social matters attests the permanent value of the Church's teaching at the same time as it attests the true meaning of her Tradition, always living and active" (no. 2421).

For over a century, the Church has witnessed an extraordinary growth in its social teaching. Most theologians trace the modern phase of Catholic social teaching back to Pope Leo XIII. In 1891 Pope Leo wrote the ground-breaking encyclical letter *On the Condition of Workers* (*Rerum Novarum*). In this teaching letter, the pope addressed the terrible exploitation and poverty of European and North American workers at the beginning of the industrial era. The encyclical inaugurated a rich period of social teaching by popes, the Second Vatican Council, bishops' conferences, and individual bishops.

In the wake of *Rerum Novarum*, the Church has developed a coherent body of social teaching on the challenges faced by modern societies. Pope Pius XI memorialized the fortieth anniversary of *Rerum Novarum* in 1931 with another encyclical letter, *The Reconstruction of the Social Order* (*Quadragesimo Anno*). In it Pope Pius denounced concentrations of wealth and economic power and called for a reconstruction of social order based on subsidiarity.

Pope John XXIII celebrated the seventieth anniversary of *Rerum Novarum* in 1961 with the encyclical letter *On Christianity and Social Progress* (*Mater et Magistra*), which was followed two years later by the papal letter *Peace on Earth* (*Pacem in Terris*). In these encyclicals, Pope John affirmed the role of church as social teacher and expressed profound concerns for the growing gap between rich and poor nations, the plight of farmers and rural areas, and the arms race. He also articulated a comprehensive vision of human rights.

The Second Vatican Council promulgated the *Pastoral Constitution on the Church in the Modern World* (*Gaudium et Spes*) in 1965. This landmark document of the world's bishops in union with the Holy Father articulates a vision of the Church engaged with the world on a wide range of social issues. The *Constitution* calls upon Catholics to protect human life, promote human dignity, and pursue genuine peace.

Pope Paul VI called "development" the new name for "peace" in his 1967 encyclical *On the Development of Peoples* (*Populorum Progressio*). He marked the eightieth anniversary of Pope Leo's *Rerum Novarum* in 1971 with the apostolic letter *A Call to Action* (*Octogesima Adveniens*). In it Pope Paul advocated for integral human development, criticized unjust economic structures and excessive inequality, and called on all Christians to work for social and political reform. Also in 1971, the World Synod of Bishops issued *Justice in the World*, which declared that "action on behalf of justice and participation in the transformation of the world fully appear to us as a constitutive dimension of the preaching of the Gospel."[1]

Pope John Paul II observed the ninetieth anniversary of *Rerum Novarum* in 1981 with the encyclical letter *On Human Work* (*Laborem Exercens*). Seven years later, he wrote another encyclical, *On Social Concern* (*Sollicitudo Rei Socialis*). In his 1991 encyclical letter, *On the Hundredth Anniversary of "Rerum Novarum"* (*Centesimus Annus*), he

reaffirmed and built upon the principles of *Rerum Novarum*. In these letters, Pope John Paul II championed the payment of just wages, the right of workers to organize, and the priority of labor over capital. He critiqued the rivalry between the nations of the West and the East as a structure of sin that compromises the progress of poor nations, and he called instead for solidarity between the wealthier nations of the North and the poorer nations of the South. He pointed out both the failures of communism and the limitations of capitalism. He upheld the rights of workers and the importance of economic initiative.

In the 1995 encyclical *The Gospel of Life* (*Evangelium Vitae*), Pope John Paul II explored new social threats to human life and linked them to a range of old threats. He decried a growing culture of death and called for building of a culture of life. He highlighted the issues of abortion and euthanasia as being particularly serious and deplorable. He mentioned a wide array of threats to human life today, but concentrated on newer threats that insidiously undermine respect for human life.

The Catholic bishops of the United States have issued pastoral letters and numerous statements that have drawn upon the social teaching of the universal Church and have applied it to issues facing our nation. In the wake of World War I in 1919, the Administrative Committee of the National Catholic War Council issued a *Program of Social Reconstruction* in which the bishops laid out principles and recommendations for social reconstruction and reform. Decades later the bishops of our nation issued a pastoral letter called *Brothers and Sisters to Us* (1979) that addressed the legacy and scourge of racism. In *The Challenge of Peace: God's Promise and Our Response* (1983), they explored the Church's teaching on peacemaking and applied it to the issues of nuclear weapons and the arms race. They articulated major principles of Catholic social teaching regarding the economy and then addressed a number of morally significant economic issues facing the United States in *Economic Justice for All: Catholic Social Teaching and the U.S. Economy* (1986). In their 1992 document *Renewing the Earth: An Invitation to Reflection and Action on Environment in Light of Catholic Social Teaching*, the Catholic bishops of the United States looked at moral dimensions of the ecological crisis. They challenged Catholics to promote a culture of life and to work to protect human life from conception to natural death in *Living the Gospel of Life: A Challenge to American Catholics* (1998). In addition, every four years since 1976, before each presidential election, the bishops have issued a statement on Catholic citizenship. (The 2003 statement is called *Faithful Citizenship: A Catholic Call to Political Responsibility*.)

This short survey of papal, conciliar, and episcopal teaching in the modern era does not do justice to the depth and breadth of the Church's social teaching. There are dozens of other examples of the Church's official teaching on social issues by popes, synods of bishops, and national bishops' conferences around the world. Some of these can be found in the "Resources on Catholic Social Teaching" section at the end of this guide. In addition, applications of the teaching to hundreds of national and international concerns can be found in documents of the Vatican, in addresses of popes and Vatican officials, and in statements and pastoral letters of bishops.

Catholic social teaching has not been expressed only in the Church's official statements. Catholic social thought also has taken shape in the writings of the ancient doctors of the Church, and it is explored today in the work of modern theologians. It is shaped and lived out by countless lay and religious men and women in their struggles to walk in the footsteps of Jesus as they seek to embody God's justice and peace in our world. The *In the Footsteps of Jesus: Catholic Social Teaching at Work Today* video (2003) and resource manual (2004) from the United States Conference of Catholic Bishops are simply primers in Catholic social teaching. By exploring seven basic themes, Catholics can become familiar with the existence and basic message of Catholic social teaching. Hopefully, this exposure to the teaching will lead them to desire to learn more about this rich doctrinal tradition and to find more ways to live it out in their lives.

Seven Themes
of Catholic Social Teaching

Following are excerpts from *Sharing Catholic Social Teaching: Challenges and Directions* (Washington, DC: USCCB, 1998) and from *Faithful Citizenship: A Catholic Call to Political Responsibility* (Washington, DC: USCCB, 2003).

LIFE AND DIGNITY OF THE HUMAN PERSON

"In a world warped by materialism and declining respect for human life, the Catholic Church proclaims that human life is sacred and that the dignity of the human person is the foundation of a moral vision for society. Our belief in the sanctity of human life and the inherent dignity of the human person is the foundation of all the principles of our social teaching. . . . We believe that every person is precious, that people are more important than things, and that the measure of every institution is whether it threatens or enhances the life and dignity of the human person." (*Sharing Catholic Social Teaching*, 4)

"Catholic teaching calls on us to work to avoid war. Nations must protect the right to life by finding ever more effective ways to prevent conflicts from arising, to resolve them by peaceful means, and to promote post-conflict reconstruction and reconciliation." (*Faithful Citizenship*, 18)

CALL TO FAMILY, COMMUNITY, AND PARTICIPATION

"In a global culture driven by excessive individualism, our tradition proclaims that the person is not only sacred but also social. How we organize our society—in economics and politics, in law and policy—directly affects human dignity and the capacity of individuals to grow in community. The family is the central social institution that must be supported and strengthened, not undermined." (*Sharing Catholic Social Teaching*, 4)

"We believe people have a right and a duty to participate in society, seeking together the common good and well-being of all. . . . Our Church teaches that the role of government and other institutions is to protect human life and human dignity and promote the common good." (*Sharing Catholic Social Teaching*, 5)

RIGHTS AND RESPONSIBILITIES

"In a world where some speak mostly of 'rights' and others mostly of 'responsibilities,' the Catholic tradition teaches that human dignity can be protected and a healthy community can be achieved only if human rights are protected and responsibilities are met. Therefore, every person has a fundamental right to life and a right to those things required for human decency. Corresponding to these rights are duties and responsibilities—to one another, to our families, and to the larger society. While public debate in our nation is often divided between those who focus on personal responsibility and those who focus on social responsibilities, our tradition insists that both are necessary." (*Sharing Catholic Social Teaching*, 5)

OPTION FOR AND WITH THE POOR AND VULNERABLE

"In a world characterized by growing prosperity for some and pervasive poverty for others, Catholic teaching proclaims that a basic moral test is how our most vulnerable members are faring. In a society marred by deepening divisions between rich and poor, our tradition recalls the story of the Last Judgment (Mt 25:31-46) and instructs us to put the needs of the poor and vulnerable first." (*Sharing Catholic Social Teaching*, 5)

THE DIGNITY OF WORK AND THE RIGHTS OF WORKERS

"In a marketplace where too often the quarterly bottom line takes precedence over the rights of workers, we believe that the economy must serve people, not the other way around. Work is more than a way to make a living; it is a form of continuing participation in God's creation. If the dignity of work is to be protected, then the basic rights of workers must be respected—the right to productive work, to decent and fair wages, to organize and join unions, to private property, and to economic initiative. Respecting these rights promotes an economy that protects human life, defends human rights, and advances the well-being of all." (*Sharing Catholic Social Teaching*, 5)

SOLIDARITY

"We are one human family. We are our brothers' and sisters' keepers, wherever they may be. Pope John Paul II insists, 'We are *all* really responsible *for all*.' Loving our neighbor has global dimensions in a shrinking world. At the core of the virtue of solidarity is the pursuit of justice and peace. Pope Paul VI taught that 'if you want peace, work for justice.' The Gospel calls us to be 'peacemakers.' Our love for all our sisters and brothers demands that we be 'sentinels of peace' in a world wounded by violence and conflict." (*Faithful Citizenship*, 15)

CARE FOR GOD'S CREATION

"On a planet conflicted over environmental issues, the Catholic tradition insists that we show our respect for the Creator by our stewardship of creation. Care for the earth is not just an Earth Day slogan; it is a requirement of our faith. We are called to protect people and the planet, living our faith in relationship with all of God's creation. This environmental challenge has fundamental moral and ethical dimensions that cannot be ignored." (*Sharing Catholic Social Teaching*, 6)

Essay
Life and Dignity of the Human Person

Human life is sacred and human dignity is the foundation of a moral vision of society. . . . The Catholic Church proclaims that human life is sacred, that it is a gift from God, and that the dignity of the human person is the foundation of a moral vision for society. Our belief in the sanctity of human life and inherent dignity of the human person is the bedrock of Catholic social teaching. In our society, human life is under direct attack from abortion and assisted suicide. The value of human life is being threatened by increasing use of the death penalty. Forty-three thousand people die of hunger and its consequences every day. We believe that every person is precious, that people are more important than things, and that the measure of every institution is whether it threatens or enhances the life and dignity of the human person. (Excerpt from the video *In the Footsteps of Jesus: Catholic Social Teaching at Work Today* [Washington, DC: USCCB, 2003])

The story of creation teaches us that the human person is created in the image and likeness of God (see Gn 1:22-27). Scripture urges us to "choose life" by the way that we live (see Dt 30:19). It is significant that the admonition of Deuteronomy appears in a book that outlines many social laws that govern the justice of the ancient Hebrew nation. God's way of life is both a personal call to integrity and a social call to fashion a society that respects human life and dignity. The Psalmist reminds us of the glory of human dignity: "What are humans that you are mindful of them, / mere mortals that you care for them? / Yet you have made them little less than a god, / crowned them with glory and honor" (Ps 8:5-6).

The Good News of the Gospel is that in Christ God has taken on our humanity and offered every person salvation. In Jesus of Nazareth the eternal Word of God became flesh and dwelt among us (see Jn 1:14). He came "that [we] might have life and have it more abundantly" (Jn 10:10). Jesus assures us, "And when I am lifted up from the earth, I will draw everyone to myself" (Jn 12:32).

Human worth is intrinsic; it is built into the fabric of human life by God. We believe that every human life is precious from conception through natural death. Our basic human dignity comes from God, not from any human quality or accomplishment. All our social structures and practices are meant to serve human dignity. Every social decision and institution must be judged in light of whether it protects or undermines the life and dignity of the human person. Every public law and program, every corporate policy and practice, every cultural pattern and social institution are subject to these moral tests: Does it protect or threaten human life? Does it uphold or undermine human dignity?

The value of human life leads to a commitment to peace. Nations must protect human life by avoiding war and by promoting justice and peace.

The theme of human life and dignity affirms an important American perspective: the value we place on the individual. But this principle also challenges our society. How will we protect in law the right to life of all, especially at life's vulnerable beginning and end? What will we do to root out the vestiges of prejudice, racism, and sexism in our social institutions? How will we expand social and economic opportunities to all racial and ethnic groups, including Blacks, Native Americans, and Hispanics? How will we extend the American dream to all persons regardless of their social status, including refugees and immigrants, the poor, and the powerless? These and other questions arise from a commitment to human life and dignity.

Scripture and Tradition
Life and Dignity of the Human Person

SCRIPTURE: GENESIS 1:26-31

Then God said: "Let us make man in our image, after our likeness. Let them have dominion over the fish of the sea, the birds of the air, and the cattle, and over all the wild animals and all the creatures that crawl on the ground."

God created man in his image; / in the divine image he created him; / male and female he created them.

God blessed them, saying: "Be fertile and multiply; fill the earth and subdue it. Have dominion over the fish of the sea, the birds of the air, and all the living things that move on the earth." God also said: "See, I give you every seed-bearing plant all over the earth and every tree that has seed-bearing fruit on it to be your food; and to all the animals of the land, all the birds of the air, and all the living creatures that crawl on the ground, I give all the green plants for food." And so it happened. God looked at everything he had made, and he found it very good. Evening came, and morning followed—the sixth day.

Other Scripture passages on the theme of the life and dignity of the human person:

Psalm 8:5-7 (humans made "little less than a god")
Deuteronomy 30:19 (choose life)
John 12:32 (Christ will draw all to himself)
1 Corinthians 15:22 (Christ died for all)

RELATED EXCERPTS FROM CATHOLIC SOCIAL TEACHING

"Furthermore, whatever is opposed to life itself, such as any type of murder, genocide, abortion, euthanasia, or willful self-destruction, whatever violates the integrity of the human person . . . whatever insults human dignity, such as subhuman living conditions, arbitrary imprisonment, deportation, slavery, prostitution, the selling of women and children; as well as disgraceful working conditions, where men are treated as mere tools for profit, rather than as free and responsible persons; all these things and others of their like are infamies indeed. They poison human society . . .

Moreover, they are a supreme dishonor to the Creator." (Second Vatican Council, *Pastoral Constitution on the Church in the Modern World* [*Gaudium et Spes*], 1965, no. 27. In *The Documents of Vatican II*, ed. Walter M. Abbott, SJ [Chicago: Follett Publishing Company, 1966].)

"Every individual, precisely by reason of the mystery of the Word of God who was made flesh (cf. Jn 1:14), is entrusted to the maternal care of the Church. Therefore every threat to human dignity and life must necessarily be felt in the Church's very heart; it cannot but affect her at the core of her faith in the Redemptive Incarnation of the Son of God, and engage her in her mission of proclaiming the *Gospel of life* in all the world and to every creature (cf. Mk 16:15)." (Pope John Paul II, *The Gospel of Life* [*Evangelium Vitae*] [Washington, DC: USCCB, 1995], no. 3)

"In a world warped by materialism and declining respect for human life, the Catholic Church proclaims that human life is sacred and that the dignity of the human person is the foundation of a moral vision for society. Our belief in the sanctity of human life and the inherent dignity of the human person is the foundation of all the principles of our social teaching. . . . We believe that every person is precious, that people are more important than things, and that the measure of every institution is whether it threatens or enhances the life and dignity of the human person." (United States Conference of Catholic Bishops, *Sharing Catholic Social Teaching: Challenges and Directions* [Washington, DC: USCCB, 1998], 4)

"We live the Gospel of Life when we live in solidarity with the poor of the world, standing up for their lives and dignity. Yet abortion and euthanasia have become preeminent threats to human dignity because they directly attack life itself, the most fundamental human good and the condition for all others. They are committed against those who are weakest and most defenseless, those who are genuinely 'the poorest of the poor.'" (United States Conference of Catholic Bishops, *Living the Gospel of Life: A Challenge to American Catholics* [Washington, DC: USCCB, 1998], 4)

Essay
Call to Family, Community, and Participation

Human beings are social beings. Our participation in our families, our communities, and in society is a reflection of our faith. . . . The person is not only sacred but also social. How we organize our society—in economics and politics, in law and policy—directly affects human dignity and the capacity of individuals to grow in community. We believe the family is the central social institution that must be supported and strengthened. We also believe people have a right and a duty to participate in social, economic, and political life. (Excerpt from the video In the Footsteps of Jesus: Catholic Social Teaching at Work Today [Washington, DC: USCCB, 2003])

The second theme of Catholic social teaching is intimately related to the first. Human dignity can be realized and protected only in community. We are social beings. Human life and dignity do not exist in isolation from the society in which we live. This truth about the social nature of human beings is woven throughout the Bible and Catholic teaching.

The Scriptures present a thoroughly social vision of humanity. God does not call us merely as individuals without relationships and mutual responsibilities. In the Scriptures God called the ancient Israelites as a people—a community, a nation, God's own people. God's covenant was not made with individuals apart from the community in which they lived. Moses ratified the covenant with blood in an assembly of the people (see Ex 24:3-8) and proscribed that God's covenant be renewed periodically "in the presence of all Israel" (Dt 31:11).

God's covenant with Israel included a whole body of social laws to protect human dignity, including laws protecting migrants, widows, orphans, and debtors; laws ensuring just judgments; laws governing fair commerce and protecting laborers; and laws providing for the needs of poor persons (see Lv 19:9-15, 35-37 and Dt 14:22-29; 15:1-18; 24:10-22).

The ancient Israelites, under the inspiration of God, remembered well their own poverty and oppression in Egypt and worked to fashion a more just society

(see Ex 22:20-22). Israel was not always faithful to God's demand for social justice. The Hebrew prophets repeatedly reminded the nation that it would be judged by the measure of its own justice as a society (for example, see Jer 7:1-7).

Jesus understood the social nature of the human person. Jesus preached and inaugurated the Reign of God, a social image and reality. He founded the Church, a community. He didn't write a "self-improvement" book. The early Church carefully structured its communal life to meet the needs of all. It even established the order of deacon to serve the social mission of the Church (see Acts 2:42-47; 4:32-35; 6:1-7).

We are indeed social beings. Human dignity and potential are only developed—and the common good is advanced—through social interaction. Our language, thought patterns, and abilities are developed through social immersion. A whole host of social institutions exist to express human dignity and promote human development, including: schools, hospitals, the arts, transportation, businesses, and health clubs. Social laws, structures, and institutions have a profound impact on human development and dignity. A key question is whether or not all persons have access or can participate in the institutions of society that are necessary for human life to grow and prosper. In the Catholic tradition, helping to shape a just society through our participation in political life is a moral obligation.

Among all of these social realities, marriage and the family hold a special place. The family is the basic cell of society, the basic community. These communities of intimacy are the basis for truly human social life. Families come in many shapes and sizes, but they have the same functions: to bring into the world and nurture human life and to enable their members to contribute to the common good of the broader society.

What cannot be accomplished at the most basic levels of society to defend and promote human life and the common good must be done at higher levels. The Church calls this *socialization*. At the same time, higher levels of social organization must be careful not to weaken or supplant lower levels; their task is to support families and local communities. This is the Church's principle of *subsidiarity*.

In the Catholic social vision, government has a special responsibility to look after the "common good." The common good comprises those social conditions that allow families and other social institutions to function in a healthy way so that persons can achieve their human potential.

The call to family, community, and participation affirms our American emphasis on teamwork, but at the same time this theme challenges our nation. How will we ensure that our public and corporate policies are pro-family and defend the institution of marriage? In a society profoundly skeptical of government, what will we do to help our country to shape the legitimate role of government (local, state, and national) in promoting the common good? How can we help our political, cultural, economic, and social institutions to examine these essential questions: What do they do to people? What do they do for people? How are people given access to them?

Scripture and Tradition
Call to Family, Community, and Participation

They devoted themselves to the teaching of the apostles and to the communal life, to the breaking of the bread and to the prayers. Awe came upon everyone, and many wonders and signs were done through the apostles. All who believed were together and had all things in common; they would sell their property and possessions and divide them among all according to each one's need. Every day they devoted themselves to meeting together in the temple area and to breaking bread in their homes. They ate their meals with exultation and sincerity of heart, praising God and enjoying favor with all the people. And every day the Lord added to their number those who were being saved.

Other Scripture passages on the theme of the call to family, community, and participation:

Genesis 17:7-8 (God's covenant with a people)
Exodus 6:6-8 (God's covenant frees a people)
Leviticus 19:9-15, 35-37 (some of the covenant's social laws)
Deuteronomy 14:22-29; 15:1-18; 24:10-22 (some of the covenant's social laws)
Psalm 72:1-30 (the just and peaceful realm)
Jeremiah 32:38-40 (God's covenant with a people and their children)
Mark 1:14-15 (the Reign of God, a social image)
Matthew 19:3-6 (marriage)
Luke 22:14-20, 1 Corinthians 11:23-26, Hebrews 8:7-12 (Christ's new covenant)

RELATED EXCERPTS FROM CATHOLIC SOCIAL TEACHING

"The State must not absorb the individual or the family; both should be allowed free and untrammelled action so far as is consistent with the common good and the interest of others." (Pope Leo XIII, *On the Condition of Labor* [*Rerum Novarum*], 1891 [available online at *www.vatican.va*], no. 35)

"The State. . . . has also the duty to protect the rights of all its people, and particularly of its weaker members, the workers, women and children. It can never be right for the State to shirk its obligation of working actively for the betterment of the condition of the workingman." (Pope John XXIII, *Christianity and Social Progress* [*Mater et Magistra*], 1961 [available online at *www.vatican.va*], no. 20)

"It is necessary to go back to seeing the family as the *sanctuary of life*. The family is indeed sacred: it is the place in which life—the gift of God—can be properly welcomed and protected against the many attacks to which it is exposed, and can develop in accordance with what constitutes authentic human growth. In the face of the so-called culture of death, the family is the heart of the culture of life." (Pope John Paul II, *On the Hundredth Anniversary of "Rerum Novarum"* [*Centesimus Annus*] [Washington, DC: USCCB, 1991], no. 39)

"In a global culture driven by excessive individualism, our tradition proclaims that the person is not only sacred but also social. How we organize our society—in economics and politics, in law and policy—directly affects human dignity and the capacity of individuals to grow in community. The family is the central social institution that must be supported and strengthened, not undermined. . . . We believe people have a right and a duty to participate in society, seeking together the common good and well-being of all. . . . Our Church teaches that the role of government and other institutions is to protect human life and human dignity and promote the common good." (United States Conference of Catholic Bishops, *Sharing Catholic Social Teaching: Challenges and Directions* [Washington, DC: USCCB, 1998], 4-5)

"In the Catholic tradition, responsible citizenship is a virtue; participation in the political process is a moral obligation." (United States Conference of Catholic Bishops, *Faithful Citizenship: A Catholic Call to Political Responsibility* [Washington, DC: USCCB, 2003], 9)

Essay
Rights and Responsibilities

Every person not only has a fundamental right to life, but also a right to those things required for human decency. . . . The Catholic tradition teaches that human dignity can be safeguarded and a healthy community achieved only if human rights are protected and responsibilities are met. Every person, therefore, has a fundamental right to life and a right to those things required for human decency. Aligned with these rights are duties and responsibilities—to one another, to our families, and to the larger society. (Excerpt from the video *In the Footsteps of Jesus: Catholic Social Teaching at Work Today* [Washington, DC: USCCB, 2003])

All people have a right to participate in the life of society. Human rights are the minimum conditions for life in community. The Church today champions a range of human rights that flow from the biblical understanding of covenant and Jesus' consistent outreach to those at the margins of society.

The prophet Isaiah decried Israel's unfaithfulness to their covenant with God in these words: "Woe to those who enact unjust statutes / and who write oppressive decrees, / depriving the needy of judgment / and robbing my people's poor of their rights, / making widows their plunder, / and orphans their prey!" (Is 10:12).

Human rights flow from our God-given human dignity. In the modern era, the Church has come to recognize three sets of basic human rights in Catholic social teaching:

1. *The right to life,* which is the foundation for all others and implies the right to food, clothing, shelter, rest, medical care, and the necessary social services.

2. *Economic rights,* which include rights to education, employment and opportunities for advancement, and the right to security in situations of sickness, old age, disability and unemployment.

3. *Political and cultural rights,* which include the right to personal respect, to immigrate, to have a family, and to freedom of conscience, expression, and assembly.

The Church recognizes that with rights come responsibilities. We each have duties to one another and to our families, to respect the rights of others and to work for the common good of all. We not only have a right to basic education and adequate employment, but we also have a responsibility to pursue them with integrity. By exercising our economic rights, we contribute to the goods and services of our society, enabling us to support our families, to strengthen the common good, and to help society meet its obligations to the poor and the vulnerable.

The Church's emphasis on human rights affirms our nation's emphasis on political rights and freedom of expression and assembly; but it also challenges us to recognize the right to life and economic rights. How will we enable our nation to embrace a consistent ethic of life "from womb to tomb"? What can we do to ensure that all citizens have access to life's basic necessities of food, clothing, housing, and medical care? How can we shape a society where all persons have access to good education and employment opportunities? And what can we do to provide for the economic security of disabled persons, the sick, and the unemployed?

Scripture and Tradition
Rights and Responsibilities

SCRIPTURE: ISAIAH 10:1-2

Woe to those who enact unjust statutes / and who write oppressive decrees, / depriving the needy of judgment / and robbing my people's poor of their rights, / making widows their plunder, / and orphans their prey!

Other Scripture passages on the theme of rights and responsibilities:

Deuteronomy 5:17; 30:19 (right to life)
Sirach 34:22 (rights of workers)
Psalm 146:5-8 (freedom from oppression)

RELATED EXCERPTS FROM CATHOLIC SOCIAL TEACHING

"But first we must speak of man's rights. Man has the right to live. He has the right to bodily integrity and to the means necessary for the proper development of life, particularly food, clothing, shelter, medical care, rest, and, finally, the necessary social services. In consequence, he has the right to be looked after in the event of ill health; disability stemming from his work; widowhood; old age; enforced unemployment; or whenever through no fault of his own he is deprived of the means of livelihood." (Pope John XXIII, *Peace on Earth* (*Pacem in Terris*) [Washington, DC: USCCB, 1963], no. 11)

"[The Catholic tradition calls for] *a society of free work, of enterprise and of participation.* Such a society is not directed against the market, but demands that the market be appropriately controlled by the forces of society and by the State, so as to guarantee that the basic needs of the whole of society are satisfied." (Pope John Paul II, *On the Hundredth Anniversary of "Rerum Novarum"* [*Centesimus Annus*] [Washington, DC: USCCB, 1991], no. 35)

"In a world where some speak mostly of 'rights' and others mostly of 'responsibilities,' the Catholic tradition teaches that human dignity can be protected and a healthy community can be achieved only if human rights are protected and responsibilities are met. Therefore, every person has a fundamental right to life and a right to those things required for human decency. Corresponding to these rights are duties and responsibilities—to one another, to our families, and to the larger society. While public debate in our nation is often divided between those who focus on personal responsibility and those who focus on social responsibilities, our tradition insists that both are necessary." (United States Conference of Catholic Bishops, *Sharing Catholic Social Teaching: Challenges and Directions* [Washington, DC: USCCB, 1998], 5)

Essay
Option for and with the Poor and Vulnerable

A basic moral test of any society is how our most vulnerable members are faring. . . . In a world marred by deepening divisions between rich and poor, our tradition recalls the story of the Last Judgment. There, we are instructed to show special concern for the poor and vulnerable because their needs are the greatest. (Excerpt from the _In the Footsteps of Jesus: Catholic Social Teaching at Work Today_ [Washington, DC: USCCB, 2003])

All members of society and society as a whole have a special obligation to poor and vulnerable persons. God's covenant with ancient Israel included a special concern for poor and vulnerable persons. This concern found expression in their communal laws: laws protecting aliens, widows, and orphans; laws protecting debtors; laws promoting just judgments; laws mandating the gleaning of the fields for the benefit of poor persons; and laws providing for the needs of poor persons from a communal tithe.

Israel's own experience of Egyptian oppression left a deep impression on the people. In Deuteronomy, we read, "You shall not defraud a poor and needy hired servant, whether he be one of your own countrymen or one of the aliens who live in your communities. . . . You shall not violate the rights of the alien or of the orphan, nor take the clothing of a widow as a pledge. For, remember, you were once slaves in Egypt, and the Lord, your God, ransomed you from there; that is why I command you to observe this rule" (Dt 24:14, 17-18). When Israel did not live up to the spirit and letter of the law, prophets arose to defend the rights of the poor.

Jesus had a special regard for poor and outcast persons. In the memorable image of the final judgment, the king separates the sheep from the goats based upon their treatment of the poorest and most vulnerable members of the community (see Mt 25:31-46). Jesus understood his own mission in special relationship to poor and outcast persons. At the beginning of his public ministry, he announced, "The Spirit of the Lord is upon me, / because [God] has anointed me / to bring glad tidings to the poor" (Lk 4:18).

The Church makes a fundamental "option for the poor" in the belief that the measure of the justice of a society is how those who are poor or vulnerable are faring. This option does not pit one socioeconomic group against another. Meeting the needs of the poorest and most vulnerable members of society strengthens the whole community and ensures that all are protected. Poverty destroys human potential and impoverishes the whole community; it breeds despair and violence to the detriment of the whole society.

The Church's option for the poor affirms our American identification with the underdog, but it also challenges many of our prejudices regarding poor persons. We often prefer to think of poor persons as lazy, to look down on them, and to blame them for their poverty.

The option for the poor raises many questions: How can we challenge ourselves to see Christ in the poor and in the vulnerable? What can we do to affirm the dignity of the poor and to give them a hand up? How can we extend our democratic ideals from the political sphere to economic life? What can we do to protect the vulnerable and empower those who are poor and powerless? How can we reduce the growing ranks of working poor families?

Scripture and Tradition
Option for and with the Poor and Vulnerable

SCRIPTURE: LUKE 4:16-20

He came to Nazareth, where he had grown up, and went according to his custom into the synagogue on the sabbath day. He stood up to read and was handed a scroll of the prophet Isaiah. He unrolled the scroll and found the passage where it was written: "The Spirit of the Lord is upon me, / because he has anointed me / to bring glad tidings to the poor. / He has sent me to proclaim liberty to captives / and recovery of sight to the blind, / to let the oppressed go free, / and to proclaim a year acceptable to the Lord." Rolling up the scroll, he handed it back to the attendant and sat down, and the eyes of all in the synagogue looked intently at him. He said to them, "Today this scripture passage is fulfilled in your hearing."

Other Scripture passages on the theme of the option
for the poor and vulnerable:

Exodus 22:20-22; Leviticus 19:33-34; Deuteronomy 24:17-18 (laws protecting aliens, widows, orphans)

Exodus 22:24-26; Leviticus 25:23-28; Deuteronomy 15:1-11; 23:20; 24:6, 10-13 (laws protecting debtors)

Deuteronomy 14:28-29; 26:12-13 (laws providing for the poor)

Luke 14:12-14 (reach out to the poor and vulnerable)

Matthew 25:31-46 (judgment of nations)

James 2:1-5, 9 (dishonor not the poor)

RELATED EXCERPTS FROM CATHOLIC SOCIAL TEACHING

"Still, when there is question of defending the rights of individuals, the poor and badly off have a claim to especial consideration. The richer class have many ways of shielding themselves, and stand less in need of help from the State; whereas the mass of the poor have no resources of their own to fall back upon, and must chiefly depend upon the assistance of the State." (Pope Leo XIII, *On the Condition of Labor* [*Rerum Novarum*], 1891 [available online at *www.vatican.va*], no 37)

"'The earth belongs to everyone, not to the rich.' These words indicate that the right to private property is not absolute and unconditional. No one may appropriate surplus goods solely for his own private use when others lack the bare necessities of life." (Pope Paul VI, *On the Development of Peoples* (*Populorum Progressio*), 1967 [available online at *www.vatican.va*], no. 23)

"The prime purpose of this special commitment to the poor is to enable them to become active participants in the life of society. It is to enable *all* persons to share in and contribute to the common good. The 'option for the poor,' therefore, is not an adversarial slogan that pits one group or class against another. Rather it states that the deprivation and powerlessness of the poor wounds the whole community. The extent of their suffering is a measure of how far we are from being a true community of persons. These wounds will be healed only by greater solidarity with the poor and among the poor themselves." (United States Conference of Catholic Bishops, *Economic Justice for All: Pastoral Letter on Catholic Social Teaching and the U.S. Economy* [Washington, DC: USCCB, 1986], no. 88)

"In a world characterized by growing prosperity for some and pervasive poverty for others, Catholic teaching proclaims that a basic moral test is how our most vulnerable members are faring. In a society marred by deepening divisions between rich and poor, our tradition recalls the story of the Last Judgment (Mt 25:31-46) and instructs us to put the needs of the poor and vulnerable first." (United States Conference of Catholic Bishops, *Sharing Catholic Social Teaching: Challenges and Directions* [Washington, DC: USCCB, 1998], 5)

Essay
Dignity of Work and the Rights of Workers

Work is more than a way to make a living; it is a form of continuing participation in God's creation. If the dignity of the work is to be protected, then we must respect the basic rights of workers. Workers must have the right to productive labor, to decent and fair wages, to organize and join associations or unions, to private property, and to economic initiative. (Excerpt from video In the Footsteps of Jesus: Catholic Social Teaching at Work Today *[Washington, DC: USCCB, 2003])*

Human dignity is expressed in the dignity of work and the rights of workers. Through work we participate in God's creative activity; we express and shape our human potential.

The Scriptures are replete with references to work, labor, workers, and wages. The Scriptures begin with a description of the work of creation. God is pictured as the model laborer. For six days God labors; on the seventh, God rests (see Gn 2:2-3). We are created in the "image" of this "worker God." The second story of creation reinforces the belief that labor is essential to human nature and dignity. The human is placed in the garden "to cultivate and care for it" (Gn 2:15).

The dignity of workers was recognized in Israel's covenant with God. Israel labored in Egypt under harsh circumstances; the memory of this oppression made them sensitive to the demands of justice (see Ex 23:9; Lv 19:33-34; Dt 10:19). The Mosaic law included a number of provisions to protect the rights of workers. Sabbath laws gave laborers a weekly rest (see Ex 20:9; 23:12; 31:15; 34:21; Lv 23:3; Dt 5:13-24). Employers were required to pay just wages at the end of each day (see Lv 19:13; Dt 24:14-15). When Israel was unfaithful to the demands of the covenant, prophets railed against the injustices that arose, including those inflicted on laborers. Jeremiah pronounced, "Woe to him who builds his house on wrong, / his terraces on injustice; / who works his neighbor without pay, / and gives him no wages" (Jer 22:13).

The Christian Scriptures reinforce a concern for workers. Jesus himself worked as a carpenter (see Mk 6:3). His parable of the laborers showed he was familiar with the legal requirement to pay the agreed-upon wage at the end of the day (see Mt 20:1-16). (Of course, God turns out to be an incredibly generous employer.) He defended the Sabbath rest as being made for the benefit of people (see Mk 2:27).

Work has a threefold moral significance in Catholic social teaching. Work is the major arena for self-expression and self-realization. Work is the ordinary way to provide for ourselves and our families. Work is a principal means of contributing to the wider community and the common good. Pope John Paul II declared work the "key" to the social question in his encyclical letter *On Human Work* (*Laborem Exercens*), nos. 10-11.

Catholic social teaching holds that people have rights to decent and productive work, to just wages sufficient to support one's household in a dignified manner, to private property and economic initiative, and to free association with other workers to protect their rights collectively. The Church strongly defends the right of workers to freely choose to form unions and associations to exercise their dignity and protect their rights. The Church also endorses productive partnerships between labor and management and encourages both to move beyond strictly adversarial relationships for the common good. The bottom line for the Church is that the economy exists for people, not people for the economy.

The Church's social teaching on labor affirms our American emphasis on hard work, but it also challenges us. How can we help our society promote the creation of jobs at living wages? What can we do to counter an uncritical anti-union stance taken by many? How can we help bridge the gulf that often exists between owners and workers?

Scripture and Tradition
Dignity of Work and the Rights of Workers

SCRIPTURE: DEUTERONOMY 24:10-15, 17-18

When you make a loan of any kind to your neighbor, you shall not enter his house to receive a pledge from him, but shall wait outside until the man to whom you are making the loan brings his pledge outside to you. If he is a poor man, you shall not sleep in the mantle he gives as a pledge, but shall return it to him at sunset that he himself may sleep in it. Then he will bless you, and it will be a good deed of yours before the LORD, your God.

You shall not defraud a poor and needy hired servant, whether he be one of your own countrymen or one of the aliens who live in your communities. You shall pay him each day's wages before sundown on the day itself, since he is poor and looks forward to them. Otherwise he will cry to the LORD against you, and you will be held guilty.

You shall not violate the rights of the alien or of the orphan, nor take the clothing of a widow as a pledge. For, remember, you were once slaves in Egypt, and the LORD, your God, ransomed you from there; that is why I command you to observe this rule.

Other Scriptures on the theme of the dignity of work and the rights of workers:

Genesis 2:2-3 (God labors and rests)
Genesis 2:15 (humans cultivate the earth)
Exodus 20:9-11; 23:12; 34:21; Leviticus 23:3;
   Deuteronomy 5:12-15 (the Sabbath gave laborers rest)
Leviticus 19:13; Jeremiah 22:13; Sirach 34:22; James
   5:4 (wage justice)
Isaiah 58:3 (do not drive laborers)
Mark 6:3 (Jesus worked as carpenter)
Matthew 20:1-16 (Jesus uses wages law in parable)
Luke 10:7; Matthew 10:9-10; 1 Timothy 5:17-18
   (laborer deserves pay)
Mark 2:27 (the Sabbath is for the benefit of people)

RELATED EXCERPTS FROM CATHOLIC SOCIAL TEACHING

"All these rights, together with the need for the workers themselves to secure them, give rise to yet another right: the right of association, that is, to form associations for the purpose of defending the vital interests of those employed in the various professions. These associations are called labor or trade unions." (Pope John Paul II, *On Human Work* [*Laborem Exercens*] [Washington, DC: USCCB, 1981], no. 20)

"All people have the right to economic initiative, to productive work, to just wages and benefits, to decent working conditions, as well as to organize and join unions or other associations." (United States Conference of Catholic Bishops, *A Catholic Framework for Economic Life* [Washington, DC: USCCB, 1996], no. 5)

"In a marketplace where too often the quarterly bottom line takes precedence over the rights of workers, we believe that the economy must serve people, not the other way around. Work is more than a way to make a living; it is a form of continuing participation in God's creation. If the dignity of work is to be protected, then the basic rights of workers must be respected—the right to productive work, to decent and fair wages, to organize and join unions, to private property, and to economic initiative. Respecting these rights promotes an economy that protects human life, defends human rights, and advances the well-being of all." (United States Conference of Catholic Bishops, *Sharing Catholic Social Teaching: Challenges and Directions* [Washington, DC: USCCB, 1998], 5)

Essay
Solidarity

We are one human family, whatever our national, racial, ethnic, economic, and ideological differences. Learning to practice the virtue of solidarity means learning that "loving our neighbor" has global dimensions in an interdependent world. (Excerpt from the USCCB video *In the Footsteps of Jesus: Catholic Social Teaching at Work Today* [Washington, DC: USCCB, 2003])

The Scriptures tell us that we are one human family, sons and daughters of a loving God. This insight is a natural consequence of belief that all people are created in the image and likeness of God (see Gn 1:27). The story of the Tower of Babel conveys the religious insight that the divisions of humanity are the result of human pride and sin (see Gn 11:1-9). The history of salvation seeks to reverse these human divisions. For example, God assures Abraham that "all the nations of the earth shall find blessing" through him and his descendents (Gn 22:18). The psalmist sings of a time when God will rule all the nations (see Ps 22:28-29). The prophets paint a vision of a world of prosperity and peace for all the nations. "They shall beat their swords into plowshares / and their spears into pruning hooks; / One nation shall not raise the sword against another, / nor shall they train for war again" (Is 2:4; also see Mi 4:1-5).

Jesus of Nazareth came to save all men and women. To the surprise of many he frequently broke the taboos of his day and reached out to persons of other nations: the Samaritan woman at the well (see Jn 4:4-42), the Roman centurion (see Mt 8:5-13), and the Canaanite woman (see Mt 15:21-28). He held up the example of the Good Samaritan (see Lk 10:25-37). The message of these actions was not lost on the early Christian community.

St. Paul taught that in Christ there are no national distinctions—no distinctions between Jew and Greek and none between slave and free (see Rom 10:12; Gal 3:28). The miracle of Pentecost overcomes national divisions. In a reversal of the confusion of Babel, the coming of the Spirit enables people who speak different languages to hear the unifying message of the Gospel (see Acts 2:1-12). United

in the Spirit, the early Christian community "had all things in common" and shared them on the basis of "each one's need" (Acts 2:44-45).

The theme of solidarity expresses the Church's concerns for world peace and international development. The Church speaks of a "universal common good" that reaches beyond our nation's borders to the global community. We are one human family regardless of national, racial, ethnic, economic, or ideological boundaries. We are called to share the resources of the earth with the whole human family. Solidarity links our fates to the fates of all nations in a web of interrelationships.

Throughout the Scriptures peace is proclaimed as God's gift to us (see Jn 14:27). Peace is also God's challenge to us. Christ is our peace. We are called to be peacemakers (see Mt 5:9).

In Catholic social teaching, peace and justice are linked; in fact, they are reciprocal. Injustices lead to war; war and other forms of violence lead to poverty and injustice. Peace itself is more than the absence of war. Peace is built not upon stockpiles of weapons, but upon the firm foundation of justice. As significant as the gap is between rich and poor in our own country, it is dwarfed by the gap between developed and developing nations. Pope Paul VI called "development" the new name for "peace" and declared, "If you want peace, work for justice." Church teaching calls for multilateral disarmament and the creation of a world order or authority to mediate international disputes.

The message of solidarity affirms the multi-ethnic makeup of American society, but it also challenges our nation in profound ways. How will our nation turn away from its propensity to resort to violence to resolve problems at home as well as abroad? What can we do to change our status as the largest exporter of arms in the world? And how can we encourage our nation to devote appropriate resources to foreign aid?

Scripture and Tradition
Solidarity

SCRIPTURE: MICAH 4:1-4

In days to come / the mount of the LORD's house / Shall be established higher than the mountains; / it shall rise high above the hills, / And peoples shall stream to it: / Many nations shall come, and say, / "Come, let us climb the mount of the LORD, / to the house of the God of Jacob, / That he may instruct us in his ways, / that we may walk in his paths." / For from Zion shall go forth instruction, / and the word of the LORD from Jerusalem. / He shall judge between many peoples / and impose terms on strong and distant nations; / They shall beat their swords into plowshares, / and their spears into pruning hooks; / One nation shall not raise the sword against another, / nor shall they train for war again. / Every man shall sit under his own vine / or under his own fig tree, undisturbed; / for the mouth of the LORD of hosts has spoken.

Other Scripture passages on the theme of solidarity:
Genesis 22:17-18; Psalm 22:28-29 (save all nations)
Isaiah 2:1-4 (peace for all nations)
Romans 10:12 (no national distinctions in God)
Galatians 3:28 (all one in Christ)

RELATED EXCERPTS FROM CATHOLIC SOCIAL TEACHING:

"The solidarity which binds all men together as members of a common family makes it impossible for wealthy nations to look with indifference upon the hunger, misery and poverty of other nations whose citizens are unable to enjoy even elementary human rights. The nations of the world are becoming more and more dependent on one another and it will not be possible to preserve a lasting peace so long as glaring economic and social imbalances persist." (Pope John XXIII, *Christianity and Social Progress* [*Mater et Magistra*] 1961 [available online at *www.vatican.va*], no. 157)

"We must repeat once more that the superfluous wealth of rich countries should be placed at the service of poor nations. . . . Otherwise their continued greed will certainly call upon them the judgment of God and wrath of the poor." (Pope Paul VI, *On the Development of Peoples* [*Populorum Progressio*], 1967 [available online at *www.vatican.va*], no. 49)

"If 'development is the new name for peace,' war and military preparations are the major enemy of the integral development of peoples. . . . On the contrary, in a different world, ruled by concern for the *common good* of all humanity, or by concern for the 'spiritual and human development of all' instead of by the quest for individual profit, peace would be *possible* as the result of a 'more perfect justice among people.'" (Pope John Paul II, *On Social Concern* [*Sollicitudo Rei Socialis*] [Washington, DC: USCCB, 1987], no. 10)

"Interdependence must be transformed into *solidarity*, based upon the principle that the goods of creation *are meant for all*. That which human industry produces through the processing of raw materials, with the contribution of work, must serve equally for the good of all. . . . *Solidarity* helps us to see the 'other'—whether a *person, people or nation*—not just as some kind of instrument, with a work capacity and physical strength to be exploited at low cost and then discarded when no longer useful, but as our 'neighbor,' a 'helper' (cf. Gn 2:18-20), to be made a sharer, on a par with ourselves, in the banquet of life to which all are equally invited by God." (Pope John Paul II, *On Social Concern* [*Sollicitudo Rei Socialis*] [Washington, DC: USCCB, 1987], no. 39)

"Our culture is tempted to turn inward, becoming indifferent and sometimes isolationist in the face of international responsibilities. Catholic social teaching proclaims that we are our brothers' and sisters' keepers, wherever they live. We are one human family, whatever our national, racial, ethnic, economic, and ideological differences. Learning to practice the virtue of solidarity means learning that 'loving our neighbor' has global dimensions in an interdependent world. This virtue is described by John Paul II as 'a firm and persevering determination to commit oneself to the common good; that is to say to the good of all and of each individual, because we are all really responsible for all' (*Sollicitudo Rei Socialis*, no. 38)." (United States Conference of Catholic Bishops, *Sharing Catholic Social Teaching: Challenges and Directions* [Washington, DC: USCCB, 1998], 5-6)

Essay
Care for God's Creation

The air we breathe, the water we drink, and the land, which nourishes us, are gifts of God that we are called to respect. . . . Christian responsibility for the environment begins with appreciation of the goodness of all God's creation. When we mistreat the natural world, we diminish our own dignity. We also put at risk the dignity of every person, especially the poor and powerless. (Excerpt from the video *In the Footsteps of Jesus: Catholic Social Teaching at Work Today* [Washington, DC: USCCB, 2003])

The story of creation affirms the beauty and goodness of all creation (see Gn 1:1–2:3). Genesis also makes it clear that we do not own the world: God does. Ultimately, we are stewards charged with managing and caring for God's wondrous creation (see Gn 2:15). Our link to the earth is symbolically expressed in Genesis. Humans are made of the "clay of the ground" (Gn 2:7). We are literally "earthlings," creatures of the earth filled with the breath of God. Humans are part of creation itself. Whatever we do to the earth, we ultimately do to ourselves.

The jubilee tradition of the Hebrew Scripture calls us to "let the land lie fallow." The Scripture also makes it clear that we do not "own" the land. God is the owner; we are merely God's tenants. The land is to be treated with respect and allowed rest, not constantly exploited (see Lv 25).

Our scriptural tradition honors creation and call us to do the same. Psalm 104 praises the beauty of creation and the glory of the Creator: "How varied are your works, LORD! / In wisdom you have wrought them all; / the earth is full of your creatures. / . . . May the glory of the LORD endure forever; / may the LORD be glad in these works!" (Ps 104:24, 31). The heavens and the earth, all their creatures and humanity itself "bless the Lord" and "praise and exalt" God forever (see Dn 3:52-90).

Jesus of Nazareth stands within this Hebrew tradition of respect for God's creation. He frequently sought the solitude of the desert and lonely places in prayer (see Mt 15:23). He used many images of nature in his teaching—the fig tree, the sower, the weeds, the mustard seed, and lost sheep (see Mt 12:33-37; 13:1-9, 24-50; 18:10-14; Mk 4:1-9, 26-34; 13:28-31; Lk 8:4-8; 13:18-19; 15:1-7). Jesus spoke lovingly of the "birds of the air" and the "wild flowers" (see Mt 7:25-34; Lk 12:22-34). He spoke of himself as the vine (see Jn 15:1-17).

In Catholic social teaching, the human person and human society do not exist in a vacuum. Our destiny is bound up with the ecosystems of our planet. The Church has begun only recently to develop an emphasis on ecology and the integrity of creation in its social teaching. This evolution of the teaching is an example of the growth of the "living tradition" of the Church's teaching in response to developments in society. As the impact of humans on the ecology of our planet has become clearer, the Church has sought to shine the light of faith on the emerging issue.

The Church does not focus on ecological issues without reference to the needs of the human community. In fact, the Church is convinced that there is a profound link between how we treat people and how we treat the earth. A concern for ecology is not placed over and against a concern for human welfare. The two go together. A society that finds the earth disposable too often finds people disposable as well. This is why the Church is so concerned about how the poor are affected by the environment. In a sense, "care for God's creation" circles us back to the first theme of Catholic social teaching, the "life and dignity of the human person." One reinforces the other.

The theme of care for God's creation affirms the delight Americans take in our beautiful mountains, plains, lakes, and shores, but it also challenges our consumerism and materialism. We must ask, How can we meet the challenge of establishing a sustainable economy that provides for human needs and protects fragile ecosystems for future generations?

Scripture and Tradition
Care for God's Creation

SCRIPTURE: GENESIS 2:4-9, 15

Such is the story of the heavens and the earth at their creation.

At the time when the LORD God made the earth and the heavens—while as yet there was no field shrub on earth and no grass of the field had sprouted, for the LORD God had sent no rain upon the earth and there was no man to till the soil, but a stream was welling up out of the earth and was watering all the surface of the ground—the LORD God formed man out of the clay of the ground and blew into his nostrils the breath of life, and so man became a living being.

Then the LORD God planted a garden in Eden, in the east, and he placed there the man whom he had formed. Out of the ground the LORD God made various trees grow that were delightful to look at and good for food, with the tree of life in the middle of the garden and the tree of the knowledge of good and bad.

The LORD God then took the man and settled him in the garden of Eden, to cultivate and care for it.

Other Scripture passages on the theme of care for God's creation:

    Genesis 1:1-31 (goodness of creation)
    Psalm 104:1-35 (hymn of creation)
    Daniel 3:74-81 (all the earth blesses God)
    Hosea 4:1-3 (humans wound the earth)

RELATED EXCERPTS FROM CATHOLIC SOCIAL TEACHING

"The dominion granted to man by the Creator is not an absolute power, nor can one speak of a freedom to 'use and misuse,' or to dispose of things as one pleases. The limitation imposed from the beginning by the Creator himself . . . shows clearly enough that, when it comes to the natural world, we are subject not only to biological laws but also to moral ones, which cannot be violated with impunity." (Pope John Paul II, *On Social Concern* [*Sollicitudo Rei Socialis*] [Washington, DC: USCCB, 1987], no. 34)

"At its core, the environmental crisis is a moral challenge. It calls us to examine how we use and share the goods of the earth, what we pass on to future generations, and how we live in harmony with God's creation." (United States Conference of Catholic Bishops, *Renewing the Earth: An Invitation to Reflection and Action on Environment in Light of Catholic Social Teaching* [Washington, DC: USCCB, 1991], 1)

"On a planet conflicted over environmental issues, the Catholic tradition insists that we show our respect for the Creator by our stewardship of creation. Care for the earth is not just an Earth Day slogan; it is a requirement of our faith. We are called to protect people and the planet, living our faith in relationship with all of God's creation. This environmental challenge has fundamental moral and ethical dimensions that cannot be ignored." (United States Conference of Catholic Bishops, *Sharing Catholic Social Teaching: Challenges and Directions* [Washington, DC: USCCB, 1998], 6)

Walking
in the Footsteps of Jesus

It is not enough to talk about the teachings of Jesus and to know Catholic social teaching. We must also put them into practice. The seven themes of Catholic social teaching provide much needed guidance for individuals, communities, institutions, and governments.

As the saying goes, we cannot just "talk the talk"; we need to "walk the walk." St. James made essentially the same point in the Scriptures:

> What good is it, my brothers, if someone says he has faith but does not have works? Can that faith save him? If a brother or sister has nothing to wear and has no food for the day, and one of you says to them, "Go in peace, keep warm, and eat well," but you do not give them the necessities of the body, what good is it? So also faith of itself, if it does not have works, is dead. (Jas 2:14-17)

The *In the Footsteps of Jesus* video poses important questions for us to ponder: Where is your faith calling you to help? What gifts and talents do you have to share with others? How is God calling you to follow in the footsteps of Jesus and put his teaching into practice in the world?

The video offers some profound advice from Blessed Teresa of Calcutta. When she was asked what to do to make a difference in the world, Blessed Teresa said simply, "Just do what's in front of you." This advice encourages us to get started, but it also demands that we open our eyes and minds to see who and what are in front of us.

This advice does not mean that we just reach out to those near at hand; but it certainly says that we cannot overlook their needs. We have only to read a newspaper or listen to a newscast to see what else is also in front of us. By engaging with "what's in front of us," each of us can match our unique gifts with the unique demands of the world around us. To do what is in front of us, we need to see what is in front of us. Then we need to "walk the walk."

CHARITY AND JUSTICE

The concluding section of the video names a number of ways that we can walk in the footsteps of Jesus today. We can help in a soup kitchen, visit someone in prison, or help resettle a refugee family. We can contact legislators, work for peace, or support a local community organization that empowers low-income people to address issues that impact them. These examples illustrate two distinct yet complementary ways to put Catholic social teaching into practice: charity and justice. These two types of responses have been called the two "feet" of Christian service. We need both feet—charity and justice—to walk the walk in the footsteps of Jesus.

Catholic social teaching calls us to both charity and justice. Charity meets the immediate needs of persons and families; but charity alone does not change social structures that attack human dignity, oppress people, and contribute to poverty. Pursuing social justice helps us change oppressive social structures; but we cannot ignore the urgent needs of persons while we work for social change. Charity and justice are incomplete without each other; they are two sides of the same coin.

Charity calls forth a generous response from individuals; justice requires concerted communal action to transform institutional policies, societal laws, or unjust social situations. With our emphasis on individualism, we Americans tend to emphasize charity over justice. The challenge for Catholics is to appreciate the demands of both charity and justice.

The *Catechism of the Catholic Church* (Washington, DC: Libreria Editrice Vaticana–USCCB, 2000, 2nd ed.) reinforces the important distinction between charity and justice. "The demands of justice must be satisfied first of all; that which is already due in justice is not to be offered as a gift of charity" (no. 2446).

The *Catechism of the Catholic Church* also speaks of both personal and social sin. The "sin of the world" can "also refer to the negative influence exerted on people by communal situations and social structures that are the fruit of men's sins" (no. 408). "Sins give rise to social situations and institutions that are contrary to the divine goodness. 'Structures of sin' are the . . . effect of personal sins. They lead their victims to do evil in their turn. In an analogous sense, they constitute a 'social sin'" (no. 1869).

The reality of "social sin," which is imbedded in social structures, institutions, and laws, requires more of us than individual acts of charity; it requires works of justice. Abortion, racism, discrimination, sexism, genocide, ecological devastation, violence, pornography, and excessive economic inequality are all examples of social sin— structures of sin that also demand action for justice.

The following chart compares and contrasts charity and justice.

CHARITY
Focuses on the needs of people
Looks at individual situations
Meets immediate needs
Ameliorates symptoms of social problems
Relies on the generosity of donors

JUSTICE
Focuses on the rights of people
Analyzes social situations or structures
Works for long-term social change
Addresses underlying social causes
Relies on just laws and fair social structures

THE ART OF CATHOLIC SOCIAL TEACHING

The "ART of Catholic Social Teaching" is a simple model originally developed by the Office of Justice and Peace of the Catholic Diocese of Richmond, Virginia, to help parish life integrate charity, Catholic social teaching, and justice.

ART is an acronym that stands for <u>A</u>ct, <u>R</u>eflect, and <u>T</u>ransform. The goal of the ART process is to infuse the values and work of building God's Reign of justice and peace into our lives and world.

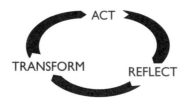

Each of these elements will be explored as we move through the model.

Act

The initial response of most people to issues of human concern is to act to meet the immediate need. For example, we feed the hungry, shelter the homeless, resettle the refugee, protect the victims of domestic violence, and recycle paper. Through this action we come in contact with the issue. The issue takes on a face; it becomes more real to us.

But this type of action alone also frustrates us. It does address the pain of people and the planet, but it does little to address its causes. People continue to come to us hungry, homeless, in flight from war and oppression, and battered. The environment continues to suffer.

Reflect

The next step is to ask why. Why are people hungry, homeless, uprooted, battered, or discriminated against? Why is the environment damaged? Why are these issues concerns of faith? What does our faith have to say about these social issues and their causes?

We begin to ask deeper questions: What factors contribute to this social problem? Who gains from the current situation? Who loses? Who has power? Who doesn't? Which beliefs and values support the status quo? And which challenge it? What does Scripture and Catholic social teaching have to say?

The *reflect* phase of the ART process enables us to explore the underlying causes of poverty, violence, homelessness, racism, war, ecological devastation, and other issues. It also gives us the opportunity to *reflect* on the rich tradition of papal, conciliar, and episcopal teaching.

Transform

The final step is to transform the social structures that contribute to suffering and injustice. Social transformation is a different kind of action. Transformation gets at root causes; it does not stop at alleviating symptoms.

We can transform our communities and our world through changing social values, empowering low-income people, advocating for just public policies, buying or boycotting goods based on social values, adopting lifestyle changes, investing in socially responsible corporations, and so forth.

The *transform* phase of ART embodies the kind of action envisioned by the World Synod of Bishops in its 1971 document *Justice in the World*: "Action on behalf of justice and participation in the transformation of the world fully appear to us as a constitutive dimension of the preaching of the Gospel, or, in other words, of the Church's mission for the redemption of the human race and its liberation from every oppressive situation" (in *Vatican Council II: More Post Conciliar Documents*, ed. Austin Flannery, OP [Northport, NY: Costello Publishing Company, Inc., 1982], 696).

The chart on the next page summarizes the "ART of Catholic Social Teaching" model and the distinction between charity and justice. Reflection on Catholic social teaching and analysis of social issues provide the link between the acts of charity and works of justice.

The ART
of Catholic Social Teaching

ACT
TRANSFORM   REFLECT

"Action on behalf of justice and participation in the transformation of the world fully appear to us as a constitutive dimension of the preaching of the Gospel, or, in other words, of the Church's mission for the redemption of the human race and its liberation from every oppressive situation." (World Synod of Bishops, *Justice in the World* (November 30, 1971), no. 6. In *Vatican Council II: More Post Conciliar Documents*, ed. Austin Flannery, OP [Northport, NY: Costello Publishing Company, Inc., 1982], 696.)

ACT *IN CHARITY* TO MEET IMMEDIATE AND URGENT NEEDS	REFLECT **ON ROOT CAUSES AND** CATHOLIC SOCIAL TEACHING	TRANSFORM *IN JUSTICE* THE ROOT SOCIAL CAUSES
• **Act** to alleviate the symptoms of social problems. Examples: Feed the hungry, shelter the homeless, resettle the refugee, reach out to persons in crisis pregnancies, protect the victims of domestic violence, and recycle paper. • Come in contact with the issue; it takes on a face. • Perform the **corporal works of mercy**: feed the hungry, give drink to the thirsty, clothe the naked, shelter the homeless, visit the imprisoned, visit the sick, and bury the dead (see Mt 25 and Tb 2).	• Ask **why**? Why are people hungry, homeless, uprooted, in crisis, battered, or discriminated against? Why is our ecosystem deteriorating? • **Listen** to those most directly affected—the poor and the marginalized. • Begin to ask deeper questions that **challenge** the status quo. • Explore the **underlying causes** of poverty, violence, homelessness, abortion, racism, ecological devastation, and other problems. • What do the **Scriptures** and **Catholic social teaching** have to say about these social issues and their causes?	• **Transform** the social structures that contribute to suffering and injustice. • To **transform** is to take a different kind of action. • **Transformative action** gets at the root causes; it does not stop at alleviating the symptoms. • **Transform** our communities and our world through working with empowered low-income people, advocating for just public policies, creating new social structures (for example, cooperatives and low-income housing), and consuming and investing in socially responsible ways.
Charity • Focuses on the needs of individuals, families, and creation • Looks at individual situations of need • Meets immediate and urgent needs • Addresses painful individual symptoms of social problems • Relies on the generosity of donors		**Justice** • Focuses on the rights of individuals, families, and creation • Analyzes social situations or social structures • Works for long-term social change • Addresses the underlying social causes of problems • Relies on just laws and fair social structures

Help for Group Facilitators and Leaders

Guide for Facilitators

The role of the facilitator is important to the successful sharing of experiences and perspectives in the group. The facilitator is not the "speaker." The role is not about having all the answers or making presentations. The video and the readings will provide the content for the discussions. The facilitator's role is simply to enable the group members to share with one another.

A good facilitator trusts the wisdom of the group. The group has the resources to make the time together supportive, insightful, and productive. The facilitator has two basic functions: to help provide support for the members of the group and to help orient the discussions of the group.

- The **SUPPORTING** function involves welcoming, attending, respecting, accepting, and invoking rules.
- The **ORIENTING** function involves preparing, initiating and modeling, guiding, clarifying, and summarizing.

Each of these functions comes naturally to some people, but each function also can be learned and improved through practice. These tasks of the facilitator are briefly described below.

Please remember that the responsibility for good sessions does not rest on the facilitator's shoulders alone. As a facilitator models these skills and functions, the other members of the group will follow the facilitator's example and contribute to the health of the group's sharing. Ultimately, it is the responsibility of the whole group to foster a supportive atmosphere in which meaningful sharing and genuine prayer can take root.

SUPPORTING

Welcoming each individual participant to the session helps to establish a supportive, non-threatening atmosphere conducive to open discussions. It is especially important for the facilitator to arrive early to set up so that he or she is available to greet each person as they arrive. It is usually helpful to provide nametags for the participants as they arrive. The facilitator should wear a nametag to model the importance of wearing one.

Welcoming includes selecting a warm and inviting room for the sessions. Set it up so that it is a welcoming space conducive to sharing. Chairs should be arranged in a circle with no "back row" seats. For this type of discussion, it is best that people not be seated at tables. A parlor arrangement is best. The participants should be seated closely together so that they can see and hear one another easily.

Finally, welcoming includes a prior consideration regarding the size of the group. Generally, the group should not be smaller than six or seven people in order to ensure adequate group dynamics. On the other hand, the group should not be larger than eleven or twelve people; otherwise group members may get lost in the "crowd," and the experience could become impersonal.

Attending to each member of the group during discussions helps to encourage participation. Participants should be invited by name to participate from time to time. Occasionally, it may be necessary to allow a pause in the discussion to ask if anyone who has not had a chance to speak has something to share.

Some specific behaviors let people know that you are attending to them. It is helpful for the facilitator to model these behaviors: making eye contact with whomever is speaking, leaning into the discussion with an open posture, and remaining relatively relaxed.

Accepting conveys respect for each member of the group. It is important for the facilitator to make it clear that there are no "right" or "wrong" responses for the purposes of these discussions. Any opinion that is expressed is accepted. Acceptance does not mean agreement with what has been said. It means accepting the person who has shared the thought, feeling, or idea. Alternate perspectives can be sought and accepted as well.

One way to convey acceptance and respect is to briefly reflect what was heard. It is helpful to briefly summarize the content of what has been said and to convey the feeling with which it was shared. Reflecting both the content and the feeling lets the person sharing know that she or he has been heard. Another way to convey respect is to allow participants to "pass" when they are not comfortable sharing a response.

Invoking rules may sound like a strange way to support the members of the group, but establishing and invoking rules can help to create a safe environment conducive to openness and sharing.

At the first session, it may be helpful to establish some ground rules for the group. The facilitator might post some sample ground rules on newsprint for the group to adopt by consensus, or the facilitator might give one example of a ground rule and invite the group to establish others. (See the section on "Avoiding Ideological Conflicts" below for additional considerations regarding ground rules.) Here are some ground rules that groups may find helpful:

We will respect confidentiality. (None of what is shared here is shared with others outside the group without getting the permission of the one who shared it.)

We will speak in the first person. (We will not speculate on what "they" think or feel.)

We will ensure the participation of all. (No one of us will dominate the discussions. We will give everyone a chance to share.)

We will not judge one another. (We may disagree, but we will accept and respect each person.)

We will follow the process. (This "rule" gives the facilitator permission to guide the discussions and to invoke the rules.)

ORIENTING

Preparing for each session will help the facilitator to orient the group to each discussion and activity. It is important for the facilitator to be familiar with the basic outline of the session so that he or she can guide the group. In addition to being familiar with the various activities and the tentative schedule, the facilitator should reflect on his or her personal responses to each question or activity in order to be prepared

to model personal sharing during the session. Finally, preparing includes collecting together any materials that will be needed during the session.

Initiating the discussions and *modeling* personal sharing are important functions of the facilitator. Initiating the discussions simply involves briefly posing a question or topic to the group. The facilitator should guard against elaborating much on the question or topic. Remember, the facilitator is not a speaker. The group only needs enough comments or instructions to orient them to the topic or process. It is the job of the members of the group to "take the ball and run with it."

Modeling personal sharing by being the first to respond to a question or exercise may be helpful. It will give other members of the group an example to follow. A good facilitator is careful to limit his or her own sharing to the amount of time that is expected of others and to present it in a way that makes it clear that these are personal reflections, not the "correct answers." It is helpful if the facilitator uses personal examples and experiences so that people are drawn to look at their own experiences. It will not be helpful if the group gets into abstract discussions instead of personal sharing. As the group becomes more comfortable with the process and with personal sharing, the facilitator may find that he or she will not need to "prime the pump" with personal reflections.

Guiding discussions is a relatively straightforward task. To help keep the group on the topic, it is helpful to occasionally restate the key question or insight under discussion. Guiding is especially helpful when the discussion seems to wander in a less-than-productive direction. It is important to guide gently, yet persistently.

Clarifying and *summarizing* are closely related to guiding. At times a good facilitator checks out what is said in the group. What are people hearing? Is that what was intended? Brief questions can help to clarify what is being said. Also, brief "what I hear you saying is this" statements can move the discussion along. Finally, good facilitators periodically summarize the key points or insights that have emerged. Such summaries give the group a sense of accomplishment and a point of reference for more sharing.

Avoiding Ideological Conflicts

Before applying Catholic social teaching to specific issues and projects, a word of caution is in order. The Church's social teaching is neither "liberal" nor "conservative." It seeks simply to be "faithful" to God's call. Church leaders in their ministerial roles should carefully avoid the appearance of being partisan or ideological. The key is to remain firmly anchored in the Church's social teaching, especially in its basic themes or principles. As specific issues are explored, people of goodwill might see complex social issues differently. Each participant in discussions should strive to be faithful to the teaching and to be respectful of others in discussing particular issues and projects.

In its *Pastoral Constitution on the Church in the Modern World* (*Gaudium et Spes*, 1965), the Second Vatican Council made an important distinction between basic moral principles and the application of these principles to specific social issues (see no. 5). The Catholic bishops of the United States made this same distinction in their pastoral letter *The Challenge of Peace: God's Promise and Our Response* (1983, see nos. 8-12).

As the Second Vatican Council taught, "Often enough the Christian view of things will itself suggest some specific solution in certain circumstances. Yet it happens rather frequently, and legitimately so, that with equal sincerity some of the faithful will disagree with others on a given matter." The Council then offered this guidance: "Hence it is necessary for people to remember that no one is allowed in the aforementioned situations to appropriate the Church's authority for his opinion. They should always try to enlighten one another through honest discussion, preserving mutual charity and caring above all for the common good."[1]

The United States Conference of Catholic Bishops echoed this teaching in *The Challenge of Peace: God's Promise and Our Response* (Washington, DC: USCCB, 1983): "On some complex social questions, the Church expects a certain diversity of views even though all hold the same universal moral principles. . . . Obviously, as bishops we believe that such differences should be expressed within the framework of Catholic moral teaching. We urge mutual respect among different groups in the Church as they analyze this letter and the issues it addresses. Not only conviction and commitment are needed in the Church, but also civility and charity" (no. 12).

The following GUIDELINES will help teachers and facilitators avoid unproductive ideological debates as groups encounter and act on Catholic social teaching.

1. Stay focused on the Church's social teaching on human life, human rights, and justice and peace, especially its basic themes and principles.
2. Acknowledge that persons of goodwill might legitimately disagree over how to apply this teaching in particular circumstances, especially in complex social situations.
3. Use the Church's social teaching as a lens to look at the moral and human dimensions of public issues.
4. Encourage dialogue and respect for the dignity of each participant in the discussion.
5. Do not allow anyone to identify the Church with a particular ideology, partisan group, political party, or candidate.
6. Over time, address a wide range of issues of concern to the Church, especially foundational issues of human life and dignity, to avoid the appearance of being ideological. Do not just focus on a few social issues of special interest to the leader.

In appropriate settings with adolescent and adult groups, teachers and facilitators might ask the group to follow some basic ground rules during their discussions. Here are some sample GROUND RULES.

1. Remember the Church's social teaching.
2. Use "I" statements. (Take responsibility for the opinions you express. Do not speak for "them.")
3. Help all to participate. (Do not dominate.)
4. Challenge ideas, not persons. (Avoid questioning the integrity or motives of others.)
5. Stay on the topic.
6. Do not identify the Church with a partisan group.
7. Be respectful and charitable at all times.

Note

1. Second Vatican Council, *Pastoral Constitution on the Church in the Modern World* (*Gaudium et Spes*), no. 43. In *The Documents of Vatican II*, ed. Walter M. Abbott, SJ (Chicago: Follett Publishing Company, 1966), 244).

Political Responsibility Guidelines for Parish Leaders

Catholics are called to be active and informed citizens. The parish has important but limited roles in the political process. These "do's" and "don'ts" for parish leaders can help guide an appropriate program of voter education prior to elections.

DO

DO share Catholic social teaching on human life, human rights, and justice and peace.

DO address the moral/human dimension of public issues.

DO apply Catholic values to legislation and public policy issues.

DO invite all candidates for public office to a Church-sponsored public forum, debate, or candidate night.

DO conduct a nonpartisan voter-registration drive on Church property.

DO encourage parishioners to vote!

DON'T

DON'T endorse or oppose candidates for political office.

DON'T distribute partisan campaign literature under church auspices or on church property.

DON'T arrange for groups to work for a candidate for public office.

DON'T invite selected candidates only to address a Church-sponsored group.

DON'T conduct voter-registration activities slanted toward one party.

DON'T distribute a biased candidate survey or a single-issue survey.

VOTER EDUCATION

For a handy review of the public issues of importance to the Catholic community, see *Faithful Citizenship: A Catholic Call to Political Responsibility* by the Administrative Committee of the United States Conference of Catholic Bishops. (Copies of the publication can be ordered by calling toll-free 800-235-8722; ask for publication no. 5-561.) Go online to *www.usccb.org/faithfulcitizenship* for additional information.

Activities

Activity
What Did Jesus Teach?

INSTRUCTIONS FOR FACILITATORS

The purpose of this exercise is to show that Jesus' teachings have relevance to today's social issues. Many youth-oriented programs ask the simple question, What would Jesus do? In the same vein, we also ask, What did Jesus teach? Of course, finding answers to these questions is not as simple as it may seem, especially for today's complex social concerns. Jesus lived in an agrarian society much different from today's information age. Nevertheless, foundational values in the teachings of Jesus can help us to solve social problems.

Be careful not to give the impression that Jesus gives simple or automatic answers to today's complex social questions. Instead show that the teachings of Jesus suggest values that guide the Church's teaching on today's issues.

The Catholic Church believes that Jesus gave the gift of the Holy Spirit to guide the Church as we confront the social issues of our day. Catholic social teaching helps the Church to be "the Body of Christ" in the world today, and it helps us to apply the teaching of Jesus to today's complex social questions.

Copy the "What Did Jesus Teach?" Scripture passages on sheets of different colors for each team. Cut the sheets of paper into slips with one Bible passage on each. Look over the descriptions of these passages to make sure that the participants cannot see the numerical references that connect the descriptions to the numbered Scripture passages.

Use the above information to introduce the exercise to the participants. Divide the group into teams of four to six individuals each. Give each team a complete set of the Bible passages for the "What Did Jesus Teach?" exercise (see pages 83-88). Ask them to spread out the passages on a desk for the entire team to read. Give them a few minutes to look them over.

Tell participants that you are looking for specific teachings of Jesus that can help the Church to grapple with particular modern social problems. Each passage is numbered, and each group has the same set of passages. The groups are to find the closest matches between teachings and issues. When they find a match, they are to simply call out the number. The first group to find a match wins a point if its members can also briefly explain how the passage speaks to the issue. (All the other groups should put aside the same numbered passage so that it is not reused.)

Make sure that participants understand the instructions. To begin, read one of the descriptions of a passage that you are looking for. The numbers of acceptable answers are in brackets after the descriptions. Do not let the participants see your list of descriptions! The first team to correctly select a passage wins the point, but a team only keeps the point if its members can explain the connection. You might prod them with these questions: What value is Jesus affirming? How can this value guide our world today?

If a group identifies another numbered passage that is not an exact match, simply say that you are looking for a closer match. Some of the passages could relate to more than one description, but the closest matches are those noted in the brackets.

Keep score and continue reading the descriptions of the teachings that you are looking for, pausing to discuss each after a passage has been matched.

A final activity to consider is asking each individual to look over all the teachings of Jesus on the slips of paper. Ask each student to select one teaching that he or she believes our world needs to put into practice at this time. Have each of them share why they selected the passage with the others.

Descriptions of Passages (to be read by teacher/facilitator)

Today many children in developing nations are forced into child labor when they should be in school. I am looking for a teaching on the value of children that suggests what Jesus would do about the rights of children and child labor laws today. [1-5]

Today many species of animals are threatened with extinction. This trend is a sign that humans are damaging the environment in ways that will ultimately hurt people, too. I am looking for a teaching that suggests that Jesus had an appreciation for animals and might share our concern today to preserve God's creatures. [41-43]

Today many older adults require special support and care as they become frail. I am looking for a teaching on caring for one's parents as they age that suggests what Jesus would do to encourage social policies that promote care for older adults. [6-7]

(NOTE: *The legal practice that Jesus is criticizing in this passage was not the regular teaching of rabbis, but it was used by some as a loophole to avoid providing support to their aging parents. By dedicating their property to a sacred purpose, they still kept ownership and use of it but got out of the obligation to use it to support their aging parents.*)

In the United States alone, more than 1.3 million children lose their lives to abortion every year. I am looking for a teaching that suggests that Jesus would defend the lives of innocent unborn children. [1-5, 43]

The Church teaches that workers deserve a just wage. I am looking for a teaching on wages that suggests what Jesus would think about promoting just wages. [22-24]

Persons who are poor often lack life's basic necessities. I am looking for a teaching on poverty that suggests how Jesus might view laws and programs designed to help those who are poor. [14-21]

Today many children in our own nation live in poverty and do not have access to basic health care services. I am looking for a teaching on the value of children that suggests what Jesus would do about the rights and needs of poor children. [1-5]

Many people today do not have health insurance or access to health care. I am looking for a teaching that suggests that Jesus would share a concern that all people have access to healing and health care. [25-26]

Medicaid is a federal program that helps families to provide low-income, older adults with nursing-home care. I'm looking for a teaching that suggests that Jesus would share a concern for caring for older adults today. [6-7]

(Note: The legal practice that Jesus is criticizing in this passage was not the regular teaching of rabbis, but it was used by some as a loophole to avoid providing support to their aging parents. By dedicating their property to a sacred purpose, they still kept ownership and use of it, but got out of the obligation to use it to support their aging parents.)

In Catholic social teaching, the family is seen as the basic building block of society. Today many people worry about the institution of the family. I am looking for a teaching on marriage that suggests that Jesus would share a concern today for strong marriages and families. [8-9]

(Note: Please be sensitive to the fact that some of the participants may come from situations of divorce. Make the point with sensitivity that the permanence of marriage remains a value that can help strengthen families.)

In the video we saw a small community in Texas that had no water. This is one example of the many ecological challenges on our planet. Others include pollution and global warming. I am looking for a teaching that suggests that Jesus had an appreciation for nature and would share the concern today for preserving God's creation. [37-40]

We live in a society that often tells us to "look after number one" (ourselves first). Many people keep to themselves in an effort not to get involved. I am looking for a teaching that suggests that Jesus would be concerned today that we work for the common good. [10-13]

Poor persons are especially vulnerable in any society. I am looking for a teaching on poverty that suggests what Jesus would think of supporting social policies today to aid the poor. [14-21]

The Church is committed to solidarity among the nations of the world. I am looking for a teaching that suggests that Jesus would share a concern for all people today regardless of their national origin. [27-29]

We live in a violent world. Often disputes between nations lead to war. The Church teaches that war should always be a last resort after we have exhausted all nonviolent attempts to resolve a dispute. I am looking for a teaching that suggests that Jesus would support strengthening nonviolent means of conflict resolution. [30-38]

World hunger and poverty are pressing problems today. I am looking for a teaching on poverty that suggests what Jesus would think of making the poor a priority in current social policies. [14-21]

Scripture Passages (photocopy and cut along lines)

---

1. Matthew 18:4-5

"Whoever humbles himself like this child is the greatest in the kingdom of heaven. And whoever receives one child such as this in my name receives me."

---

2. Matthew 19:13-14

Then children were brought to him that he might lay his hands on them and pray. The disciples rebuked them, but Jesus said, "Let the children come to me, and do not prevent them; for the kingdom of heaven belongs to such as these."

---

3. Mark 9:36-37

Taking a child he placed it in their midst, and putting his arms around it he said to them, "Whoever receives one child such as this in my name, receives me; and whoever receives me, receives not me but the one who sent me."

---

4. Luke 9:48

And said to them, "Whoever receives this child in my name receives me, and whoever receives me receives the one who sent me. For the one who is least among all of you is the one who is the greatest."

---

5. Luke 18:15-16

People were bringing even infants to him that he might touch them, and when the disciples saw this, they rebuked them. Jesus, however, called the children to himself and said, "Let the children come to me and do not prevent them; for the kingdom of God belongs to such as these."

---

6. Matthew 15:3-6

He said to them in reply, "And why do you break the commandment of God for the sake of your tradition? For God said, 'Honor your father and your mother,' and 'Whoever curses father or mother shall die.' But you say, 'Whoever says to father or mother, "Any support you might have had from me is dedicated to God," need not honor his father.' You have nullified the word of God for the sake of your tradition."

----

7. Mark 7:10-13

"For Moses said, 'Honor your father and your mother,' and 'Whoever curses father or mother shall die.' Yet you say, 'If a person says to father or mother, "Any support you might have had from me is *qorban*"' (meaning, dedicated to God), you allow him to do nothing more for his father or mother. You nullify the word of God in favor of your tradition that you have handed on. And you do many such things."

8. Matthew 19:4-6

He said in reply, "Have you not read that from the beginning the Creator 'made them male and female' and said, 'For this reason a man shall leave his father and mother and be joined to his wife, and the two shall become one flesh'? So they are no longer two, but one flesh. Therefore, what God has joined together, no human being must separate."

----

9. Mark 10:6-9

"But from the beginning of creation, 'God made them male and female. For this reason a man shall leave his father and mother [and be joined to his wife], and the two shall become one flesh.' So they are no longer two but one flesh. Therefore what God has joined together, no human being must separate."

----

10. Matthew 22:37-39

He said to him, "You shall love the Lord, your God, with all your heart, with all your soul, and with all your mind. This is the greatest and the first commandment. The second is like it: You shall love your neighbor as yourself."

----

11. Mark 12:28-31

One of the scribes, when he came forward and heard them disputing and saw how well he had answered them, asked him, "Which is the first of all the commandments?" Jesus replied, "The first is this: 'Hear, O Israel! The Lord our God is Lord alone! You shall love the Lord your God with all your heart, with all your soul, with all your mind, and with all your strength.' The second is this: 'You shall love your neighbor as yourself.' There is no other commandment greater than these."

----

12. Luke 10:27

"He said in reply, 'You shall love the Lord, your God, with all your heart, with all your being, with all your strength, and with all your mind, and your neighbor as yourself.'"

----

13. John 13:34

"I give you a new commandment: love one another. As I have loved you, so you also should love one another."

---

14. Matthew 19:21

Jesus said to him, "If you wish to be perfect, go, sell what you have and give to [the] poor, and you will have treasure in heaven. Then come, follow me."

---

15. Matthew 25:35-36

"For I was hungry and you gave me food, I was thirsty and you gave me drink, a stranger and you welcomed me, naked and you clothed me, ill and you cared for me, in prison and you visited me."

---

16. Mark 10:21

Jesus, looking at him, loved him and said to him, "You are lacking in one thing. Go, sell what you have, and give to [the] poor and you will have treasure in heaven; then come, follow me."

---

17. Luke 4:18-19

"The Spirit of the Lord is upon me, / because he has anointed me / to bring glad tidings to the poor. / He has sent me to proclaim liberty to captives / and recovery of sight to the blind, / to let the oppressed go free, / and to proclaim a year acceptable to the Lord."

---

18. Luke 6:20-21

And raising his eyes toward his disciples he said: "Blessed are you who are poor, for the kingdom of God is yours. Blessed are you who are now hungry, for you will be satisfied. Blessed are you who are now weeping, for you will laugh."

---

19. Luke 6:30-31

"Give to everyone who asks of you, and from the one who takes what is yours do not demand it back. Do to others as you would have them do to you."

---

20. Luke 12:33-34

"Sell your belongings and give alms. Provide money bags for yourselves that do not wear out, an inexhaustible treasure in heaven that no thief can reach nor moth destroy. For where your treasure is, there also will your heart be."

----

21. Luke 18:22

When Jesus heard this he said to him, "There is still one thing left for you: sell all that you have and distribute it to the poor, and you will have a treasure in heaven. Then come, follow me."

----

22. Matthew 10:9-10

"Do not take gold or silver or copper for your belts; no sack for the journey, or a second tunic, or sandals, or walking stick. The laborer deserves his keep."

----

23. Matthew 20:1-2

"The kingdom of heaven is like a landowner who went out at dawn to hire laborers for his vineyard. After agreeing with them for the usual daily wage, he sent them into his vineyard."

----

24. Luke 10:7

"Stay in the same house and eat and drink what is offered to you, for the laborer deserves his payment. Do not move about from one house to another."

----

25. Matthew 11:2-5

When John heard in prison of the works of the Messiah, he sent his disciples to him with this question, "Are you the one who is to come, or should we look for another?" Jesus said to them in reply, "Go and tell John what you hear and see: the blind regain their sight, the lame walk, lepers are cleansed, the deaf hear, the dead are raised, and the poor have the good news proclaimed to them."

----

26. Luke 7:22

And he said to them in reply, "Go and tell John what you have seen and heard: the blind regain their sight, the lame walk, lepers are cleansed, the deaf hear, the dead are raised, the poor have the good news proclaimed to them."

----

27. Luke 13:29

"And people will come from the east and the west and from the north and the south and will recline at table in the kingdom of God."

---

28. John 4:9-10

The Samaritan woman said to him, "How can you, a Jew, ask me, a Samaritan woman, for a drink?" (For Jews use nothing in common with Samaritans.) Jesus answered and said to her, "If you knew the gift of God and who is saying to you, 'Give me a drink,' you would have asked him and he would have given you living water."

---

29. John 12:32

"And when I am lifted up from the earth, I will draw everyone to myself."

---

30. Matthew 5:9

"Blessed are the peacemakers, for they will be called children of God."

---

31. Matthew 5:38-39

"You have heard that it was said, 'An eye for an eye and a tooth for a tooth.' But I say to you, offer no resistance to one who is evil. When someone strikes you on [your] right cheek, turn the other one to him as well."

---

32. Matthew 5:43-45

"You have heard that it was said, 'You shall love your neighbor and hate your enemy.' But I say to you, love your enemies, and pray for those who persecute you, that you may be children of your heavenly Father, for he makes his sun rise on the bad and the good, and causes rain to fall on the just and the unjust."

---

33. Matthew 18:21-22

Then Peter approaching asked him, "Lord, if my brother sins against me, how often must I forgive him? As many as seven times?" Jesus answered, "I say to you, not seven times but seventy-seven times."

---

34. Luke 6:27-29

"But to you who hear I say, love your enemies, do good to those who hate you, bless those who curse you, pray for those who mistreat you. To the person who strikes you on one cheek, offer the other one as well, and from the person who takes your cloak, do not withhold even your tunic."

---

35. Luke 6:37

"Stop judging and you will not be judged. Stop condemning and you will not be condemned. Forgive and you will be forgiven."

---

36. John 14:27

"Peace I leave with you; my peace I give to you. Not as the world gives do I give it to you. Do not let your hearts be troubled or afraid."

---

37. Luke 24:36

While they were still speaking about this, he stood in their midst and said to them, "Peace be with you."

---

38. Matthew 6:28-29

"Why are you anxious about clothes? Learn from the way the wild flowers grow. They do not work or spin. But I tell you that not even Solomon in all his splendor was clothed like one of them."

---

39. Luke 12:27

"Notice how the flowers grow. They do not toil or spin. But I tell you, not even Solomon in all his splendor was dressed like one of them."

---

40. Luke 13:18-19

Then he said, "What is the kingdom of God like? To what can I compare it? It is like a mustard seed that a person took and planted in the garden. When it was fully grown, it became a large bush and 'the birds of the sky dwelt in its branches.'"

---

41. Luke 21:29-31

He taught them a lesson. "Consider the fig tree and all the other trees. When their buds burst open, you see for yourselves and know that summer is now near; in the same way, when you see these things happening, know that the kingdom of God is near."

----

42. Matthew 10:29

"Are not two sparrows sold for a small coin? Yet not one of them falls to the ground without your Father's knowledge."

----

43. Luke 12:6

"Are not five sparrows sold for two small coins? Yet not one of them has escaped the notice of God."

Activity

Catholic Social Teaching Multiple Choice Quiz

1. The Church's teaching on human life and dignity leads the Church to
   a. oppose abortion as a preeminent threat to human life.
   b. oppose assisted suicide.
   c. oppose the use of the death penalty.
   d. work to end world hunger.
   e. all of the above

2. Human dignity is best promoted when
   a. each person looks out for his/her own interests.
   b. we keep the government out of people's lives.
   c. the poor are forced to improve their own lives.
   d. people work for the common good.
   e. all of the above

3. The central social institution is
   a. the individual.
   b. marriage and the family.
   c. the government.
   d. the Church.
   e. all of the above

4. People have a right to
   a. life.
   b. food and clothing.
   c. housing and health care.
   d. employment.
   e. all of the above

5. A basic moral test of society is
   a. how well the middle-class is doing.
   b. whether all people have a chance to get rich.
   c. how well the poor and the vulnerable are faring.
   d. the survival of the fittest.
   e. all of the above

6. Workers have a right to
   a. productive work.
   b. decent and fair wages.
   c. choose to organize and join unions.
   d. own private property.
   e. all of the above

7. A just wage is
   a. the rate of pay that market conditions set.
   b. what an employer can afford to pay and stay in business.
   c. enough for a family to meet its basic living expenses.
   d. what an employee agrees to accept.
   e. all of the above

8. Solidarity requires that
   a. we care about others no matter where they live or how different they appear.
   b. charity begins at home.
   c. all persons need to pull themselves up by their bootstraps.
   d. all people need to have equal incomes.
   e. all of the above

9. The Catholic view of the environment is that
   a. the natural world needs to be dominated.
   b. we must choose between jobs and the environment.
   c. mistreating the natural world hurts humanity, too.
   d. poor communities have few environmental problems.
   e. all of the above

10. The Church's social teaching calls Catholics to
    a. help the poor and vulnerable by contacting legislators.
    b. help the poor and vulnerable by getting involved in a charity.
    c. support groups that empower low-income people.
    d. make a difference in the world by using our gifts.
    e. all of the above

NOTE: The correct answers to these questions are based on official Catholic social teaching. Answer Key is on separate page.

Answer Key to Multiple Choice Quiz

1. **e.** The Church consistently defends human life.

2. **d.** The common good is the sum total of social conditions that enable people as individuals and groups to reach their human potential.

3. **b.** Marriage is the foundation and the family is the basic cell of society. Other institutions are supposed to support, not undermine, families. Government is charged with promoting the common good to create conditions in which human dignity and families can flourish.

4. **e.** The foundational right to life includes a right to all those things necessary to sustain a dignified life. With these rights come responsibilities to one's family, one's community, and the common good.

5. **c.** The poor and vulnerable have a special claim on society because their needs are greatest and their human rights are most at risk.

6. **e.** Work is a form of continuing participation in God's creation. Workers have fundamental rights.

7. **c.** The Church supports a family wage.

8. **a.** Solidarity expresses the interdependence of the human family, God's family; it requires just policies, locally, nationally, and internationally.

9. **c.** The fate of humanity is bound up with the fate of God's creation.

10. **e.** All Catholics are called to use their gifts to meet the needs of the poor and the vulnerable in charity and to transform unjust social structures in justice.

Activity
Stand Up If . . .

INSTRUCTIONS FOR FACILITATORS

The purpose of the following exercise is to demonstrate how all of us are involved in living Catholic social teaching. The exercise is meant to be non-threatening and to encourage movement, reflection, and the participants' getting acquainted with each other. The exercise is called "Stand Up If . . ." Do not provide the group with any background on the purpose of this exercise before starting. It will be more effective if you explore its purpose during the debriefing phase afterwards.

To introduce the exercise, simply say something like the following:

Today we will get started with some physical activity. It should be fun. Don't worry; it does not require any physical coordination. We will be doing the "Stand Up If. . . ." exercise. As I read each statement, simply *stand up if* it applies to you. Remain standing until I tell the whole group to sit down for the next set of exercises. You might look around to see who is standing each time. You cannot ask each other questions now, but you can always talk during the break. I promise not to make you stand for any statements that will be too revealing or embarrassing.

Ready to get started? Let's go!

Stand up if you have ever written to a soccer ball manufacturer. (Remember to remain standing!)

Stand up if you have ever personally bought a soccer ball. (Remember to remain standing!)

Stand up if you were ever with someone who was purchasing a soccer ball. (Remember to remain standing!)

Stand up if your family owns a soccer ball. (Remember to remain standing!)

Stand up if any person you know plays soccer. (Remember to remain standing!)

Stand up if you have ever heard of soccer. (Remember to remain standing!)

Now you can all sit down.

Stand up if you have ever written a letter to Congress regarding hunger assistance for developing nations or food stamps for the poor of our own nation. (Remember to remain standing!)

Stand up if you have ever attended a talk or course on world hunger—its causes and remedies. (Remember to remain standing!)

Stand up if you have ever read an article on hunger in our nation or world. (Remember to remain standing!)

Stand up if you or your family have ever contributed food or donations to a local food pantry or an international aid program. (Remember to remain standing!)

Stand up if you have ever heard of the issue of world hunger.

Okay, you can all sit now.

Stand up if you have ever met with a local or state official regarding a social justice issue. (Remember to remain standing!)

Stand up if you have ever visited a federal public official regarding a social justice issue. (Remember to remain standing!)

Stand up if you have ever written a letter to a federal, state, or local official regarding a social justice issue. (Remember to remain standing!)

Stand if you have ever written a letter to the editor of a publication regarding a social justice issue. (Remember to remain standing!)

Stand up if you have ever discussed social justice issues with family, friends, or acquaintances.

Now you can all sit down again.

Stand up if you own a business that employs people. (Remember to remain standing!)

Stand up if you are a member of a union or workers' association. (Remember to remain standing!)

Stand up if you work or have ever worked as an employee of any type of business. (Remember to remain standing!)

Stand up if you or your family have any money invested in the stock market (however much or little). (Remember to remain standing!)

Stand up if you have ever gone shopping.

Now you can sit down again.

(NOTE: The following round is more effective with adult groups of voting age.)

Stand up if you read the Catholic bishops of the United States' statement on *Faithful Citizenship* before the last federal election. (Remember to remain standing!)

Stand up if you attended a voter-education program on social issues sponsored by the Church or a civic organization before the last federal, state, or local election. (Remember to remain standing!)

Stand up if you voted in the last local election in your city or country. (Remember to remain standing!)

Stand up if you voted in the last state or federal election for the state legislature, governor, Congress, or President. (Remember to remain standing!)

Stand up if you are registered to vote. (Remember to remain standing!)

Stand up if you have ever voted. (Remember to remain standing!)

Stand up if you are not eligible to vote due to your age or country of origin.

Now you can all sit down.

DEBRIEFING

Begin by asking some open-ended questions such as these: How did you feel as we engaged in this exercise? Did you notice any patterns? Why do you think we chose to start with this exercise?

Did everyone get a chance to stand at least once? If we are like most groups, you probably got a chance to stand many times.

What does this exercise have to do with Catholic social teaching? It has a lot to do with it. In our everyday lives as consumers, owners, workers, investors, and citizens, we make decisions that impact human life, human dignity, human rights, and the care of God's creation. What we do and what we fail to do have enormous impact on the poor, the vulnerable, and the exploited.

You were probably wondering about our focus on soccer balls in the first set of questions. Tragically, at one time many soccer balls were produced with the use of child labor. If you have ever been connected with purchasing a soccer ball or have been affiliated with persons who use soccer balls, your life has touched this question. The key is, Are we conscious of the need to purchase soccer balls that are certified as *not* having been produced with child labor? Perhaps some of you are aware of this issue. All of us need to be.

The second set of statements highlights the issue of hunger. It moves from social action to address the causes of hunger, to analysis of the social factors that contribute to world hunger, and it concludes with direct service to hungry people. If we are like most groups, we tend to be involved in feeding the hungry, and we spend less time asking why there are so many hungry people and what we can to do to remove the causes of hunger.

The third and the last sets of questions focus on our activities as citizens. Are we actively involved in electing public officials and holding them accountable? Federal, state, and local public policies have an enormous impact on poor and vulnerable people. Are we protecting human life? Fostering the common good? Building world peace? Protecting the integrity of creation?

The next-to-last set of "Stand Up If" statements touch on economic life. We all participate in the economy in one way or another as owners, workers, professionals, consumers, and investors. Our decisions determine whether or not workers will make a living wage, businesses that provide employment and contribute to the common goodwill will prosper and provide employment, the environment will be protected, and fundamental human rights will be respected.

There is a certain symbolism to the "Stand Up If . . ." exercise. The study of Catholic social teaching can help make us aware of our need to "stand up" as consumers, investors, owners, workers, and citizens for the social justice values we hold as Catholics.

For an inspiring statement on how we can live Catholic social teaching every day, see the United States Conference of Catholic Bishops' statement *Everyday Christianity: To Hunger and Thirst for Justice* (Washington, DC: USCCB, 1998).

Resources on Catholic Social Teaching

Papal Social Teaching Documents

(in chronological order)

On the Condition of Labor (*Rerum Novarum*), Pope Leo XIII, 1891
This foundational document marks the beginning of modern Catholic social teaching. Pope Leo addresses the plight of workers, rejects class struggle, affirms workers' rights, and supports unions in this encyclical letter.

On the Reconstruction of the Social Order (*Quadragesimo Anno*), Pope Pius XI, 1931
Pope Pius XI commemorates the fortieth anniversary of *Rerum Novarum* with this encyclical letter that denounces the concentration of wealth and economic power and calls for the reconstruction of the social order based on subsidiarity.

Christianity and Social Progress (*Mater et Magistra*), Pope John XXIII, 1961
Seventy years after *Rerum Novarum*, Pope John XXIII affirms the role of the Church as a social teacher in this document. In it he expresses profound concerns for the growing gap between rich and poor nations, for the plight of farmers and rural areas, and for the arms race.

Peace on Earth (*Pacem in Terris*), Pope John XXIII, 1963
In this encyclical letter, Pope John XXIII affirms human rights, calls for peace based on trust and respect for these rights, urges disarmament, and supports creation of a world authority to protect the universal common good.

On the Development of Peoples (*Populorum Progressio*), Pope Paul VI, 1967
Saying that the world's poor are marginalized in this encyclical letter, Pope Paul VI calls for integral human development, criticizes unjust economic structures that lead to inequality, and calls for new international economic and social relationships in this document.

A Call to Action (*Octogesima Adveniens*), Pope Paul VI, 1971
Marking the eightieth anniversary of *Rerum Novarum* with this document, Pope Paul VI asks Christians to work for social and political reform to promote social justice. He affirms the role of individuals and local Christian communities in overcoming injustices.

Evangelization in the Modern World (*Evangelii Nuntiandi*), Pope Paul VI, 1975
In this document, Pope Paul VI articulates a "new evangelization" that links social transformation with the proclamation of the Gospel. In light of many social challenges, he calls for evangelization that transforms both individual believers and social structures.

Redeemer of Man (*Redemptor Hominis*), Pope John Paul II, 1979
In Pope John Paul II's first encyclical letter, he examines human dignity and rights in light of the mystery of redemption. He questions the adequacy of current economic and political structures to address injustices.

On Human Work (*Laborem Excercens*), Pope John Paul II, 1981
In this encyclical letter marking the ninetieth anniversary of *Rerum Novarum*, Pope John Paul II defends the dignity of work and the rights of workers. He explores just wages, the right to organize, and affirms the priority of labor over capital.

On Social Concern (*Sollicitudo Rei Socialis*), Pope John Paul II, 1987

In this encyclical letter, Pope John Paul II reaffirms the continuing tradition of the Church's social teaching. He critiques East-West blocs and other "structures of sin" that compromise the progress of poor nations. The pope calls for solidarity between rich and poor nations.

On the Hundredth Anniversary of "Rerum Novarum" (*Centesimus Annus*), Pope John Paul II, 1991

Pope John Paul II observes the centennial of *Rerum Novarum* with this encyclical letter in which he examines the failure of communism and the limitations of capitalism. He restates themes of Pope Leo's encyclical of a century before and calls for a just society based on the rights of workers, economic initiative, and participation.

The Gospel of Life (*Evangelium Vitae*), Pope John Paul II, 1995

In this encyclical letter, Pope John Paul II explores many threats to human life and some signs of hopefulness. He decries the culture of death and calls for a culture of life. The encyclical names a wide range of old and new life issues while concentrating on newer threats.

Conciliar and Synodal Documents

Constitution on the Church in the Modern World (*Gaudium et Spes*), Second Vatican Council, 1965

The Council engages the Church with the challenges of modern society. The document explores social teaching, addresses a wide range of social issues, and calls on all Christians to act in defense of human life, human dignity, and peace.

Justice in the World (*Justitia in Mundo*), World Synod of Bishops, 1971

This document locates action for justice at the heart of the Gospel (as "constitutive") and calls on the Church itself to be just if it would venture to speak to others about justice.

General Resource

Catechism of the Catholic Church, 2nd ed., 2000

Catholic social teaching is integrated throughout the text of the *Catechism*, which includes a major treatment of social teaching and various social issues in Part 3, "Life in Christ."

Documents of the United States Conference of Catholic Bishops (USCCB)*

Program of Social Reconstruction, 1919

In the wake of World War I, this document of the Administrative Committee of the bishops' conference of the United States lays out principles and recommendations for social reconstruction and reform.

Brothers and Sisters to Us, 1979

In this landmark pastoral letter, the bishops promote discussion and action against racism, "an evil which endures in our society and in our Church."

The Challenge of Peace: God's Promise and Our Response, 1983

This pastoral letter summarizes the Church's teaching on peacemaking and applies this tradition to the issues of nuclear weapons and the arms race.

Economic Justice for All: Catholic Social Teaching and the U.S. Economy, 1986

This pastoral letter summarizes major principles of Catholic social teaching regarding the economy and then addresses a number of morally significant economic issues facing the United States.

Note: In 2001 the National Conference of Catholic Bishops (NCCB) and United States Catholic Conference (USCC) became the United States Conference of Catholic Bishops (USCCB). Earlier in the twentieth century, the Catholic bishops of the United States had formed the National Catholic War Council (1917-1919), the National Catholic Welfare Council (1919-1922), and the National Catholic Welfare Conference (1922-1966).

A Century of Social Teaching: A Common Heritage, A Continuing Challenge, 1991
This brief statement summarizes six basic themes of Catholic social teaching. It was published to mark the hundredth anniversary of *Rerum Novarum*.

Renewing the Earth: An Invitation to Reflection and Action on Environment in Light of Catholic Social Teaching, 1992
This document explores many environmental challenges and is the first major treatment of the moral dimensions of the ecological crisis by the Catholic bishops of the United States.

Communities of Salt and Light: Reflections on the Social Mission of the Parish, 1993
This document is a resource for strengthening the parish's social mission and infusing social teaching into all aspects of parish life.

The Harvest of Justice Is Sown in Peace: A Reflection of the National Conference of Catholic Bishops on the Tenth Anniversary of "The Challenge of Peace," 1994
This reflection addresses the dangers of U.S. isolationism, the value of nonviolence, the just-war theory, humanitarian intervention, deterrence, conscientious objection, and the development of peoples.

Confronting a Culture of Violence: A Catholic Framework for Action, 1994
This pastoral message addresses the need for a moral revolution and a renewed ethic of justice, responsibility, and community to confront the growing culture of violence.

A Decade After Economic Justice for All: Continuing Principles, Changing Context, New Challenges, 1996
This pastoral message marks the tenth anniversary of the pastoral letter *Economic Justice for All*. Using the principles in the original pastoral, it explores contemporary economic challenges.

Called to Global Solidarity: International Challenges for U.S. Parishes, 1997
In the tradition of the bishops' *Communities of Salt and Light*, this statement calls on parishes to integrate global solidarity into all aspects of parish life.

Living the Gospel of Life: A Challenge to American Catholics, 1998
This statement challenges Catholics to promote a culture of life and to work to protect human life from conception to natural death.

Sharing Catholic Social Teaching: Challenges and Directions. Reflections of the Catholic Bishops of the United States, 1998
This statement summarizes seven major themes of Catholic social teaching and explores the importance of incorporating Catholic social teaching into Catholic educational and formational programs.

Everyday Christianity: To Hunger and Thirst for Justice, 1998
This pastoral reflection on lay discipleship in the new millennium describes and affirms the lay mission to work for justice and peace through everyday choices and commitments.

In All Things Charity: A Pastoral Challenge for the New Millennium, 1999
In this document, the bishops offer thanks and encouragement to those responding to the "cries of the poor" through the Church's works of charity, justice, and peace.

A Place at the Table: A Catholic Recommitment to Overcome Poverty and to Respect the Dignity of All God's Children, 2002
In this statement, the bishops insist that all people should have a place at the table of life. They urge Catholics to work to address continuing poverty in our land and around the world.

Faithful Citizenship: A Catholic Call to Political Responsibility, 2003

In this document, the bishops urge Catholics to "see civic and political responsibilities through the eyes of faith" and to "participate now and in the future in the debates and choices over the values, vision, and leaders that will guide our nation."

Programs and Additional Materials of the USCCB

Departments of the United States Conference of Catholic Bishops (USCCB) offer programs to help Catholics to respond to Catholic social teaching through acts of charity (service) and works of justice (social transformation). Except as noted, each department is located at 3211 Fourth Street, NE, Washington, DC 20017-1194.

USCCB Publishing
Phone: 800-235-8722
Website: *www.usccb.org/publishing*
Publishes conciliar, papal, and USCCB statements on social issues as well as other resources.

Catholic Campaign for Human Development
Phone: 202-541-3210
Website: *www.usccb.org/cchd*
The USCCB's domestic anti-poverty program makes grants to low-income community organizations and publishes prayer books, videos, study guides, and materials on Catholic social teaching, poverty, and justice.

Pro-Life Activities
Phone: 202-541-3070
Website: *www.usccb.org/prolife*
Coordinates public education and advocacy on pro-life issues and produces a manual, posters, flyers, brochures, and two newsletters on issues reflecting the Church's consistent ethic of life.

Social Development and World Peace
Phone: 202-541-3195
Website: *www.usccb.org/sdwp*
Coordinates public education and advocacy on both domestic and international issues of social justice and produces resources, manuals, and other materials to accompany bishops' statements on Catholic social teaching and issues of justice and peace.

Migration and Refugee Services
202-541-3220
Website: *www.usccb.org/mrs*
Coordinates public education and advocacy on issues touching migrants and refugees; supports a network of diocesan programs that reaches out to migrants and refugees; and produces information, materials, and videos on how to "welcome the stranger" into U.S. Catholic communities.

Catholic Relief Services (CRS)
Phone: 410-625-2220
Address: 209 West Fayette Street
Baltimore, MD 21201-3443
Website: *www.catholicrelief.org*
The USCCB's overseas development agency publishes study materials and videos and sponsors Operation Rice Bowl, a Lenten program of prayer, fasting, learning, and giving.

Notes